WITTY PUTDOWNS AND CLEVER INSULTS

RT HON PETER D ROBINSON

PR
BOOKS

PETER ROBINSON

CONTENTS

PREFACE

This book was initially structured in two parts. Part 1 comprised an analysis of the art of putdowns, its culture and psychology, then Part 2 moved into providing a wealth of examples gathered together in a compendium. In the book's final iteration, I frequently leapfrog from one dimension to the other, and back again. My thinking is that it might help to see examples of the performance of the art alongside the study of its history, purpose, and impact.

Some putdowns in this study are of uncertain origin, disputed authorship, or have multiple claimants. In my research, I therefore did not seek to credit them to any individual. I found quotes that appeared so similar to others, it made it challenging to attribute them accurately to the original parent. Indeed, I found it revealing to discover how many quotes I have heard or read, during my lifetime, were remastered from the genius of past performers. Reworking quips to suit your circumstances, of course, is something you can do as well.

I perceived that my selection of putdowns will probably reveal a lot about me; what I believe to be funny, what I intellectually consider clever and what I regard stimulating. So, I have tossed in a few 'against the grain' illustrations to confuse. What I have been unable to disguise is my 'world view'. Like the lettering in rock candy, it is so ingrained that it cannot be extracted– though it has been diminished by careful editing. Enjoy!

FIRE IN THE HOLE! THE EXPLOSIVE ART OF PUTDOWNS

As you prepare to take a fascinating trek through the minefield of verbal warfare, let me reveal and confess my rough and rowdy past. Having survived and thrived for more than forty unrelenting, spin-filled years in the snake pit of politics as a British MP, Minister, and until my retirement, as Northern Ireland's First Minister, allow me to be your seasoned tour guide behind the curtain of cunning comebacks! But before we dive into the meat of this book, I recommend, as an entrée, that we look at the elegant — or eloquently spiteful — art of the putdown.

Suppose you found yourself locked in a duel of words with that one guy who just won't shut up during meetings, the friend who morphs into a steamroller during a casual discussion, the relentless and pugnacious competitor who'd argue over the exact shade of blue in the sky, or even a political adversary with a fondness for cheap shots. What's a person in your position to do, you ask? Well, fear not! But before you launch a witty torpedo, let's consider how to do it, if at all, without sinking your own battleship.

Together, we'll journey through the labyrinth of language, uncovering a Pandora's box of persuasive dialogue. We'll study the art of distilling powerful arguments into a few well-crafted barbs, and the subtle power of empathetic engagement. It's about more than just chatterbox politics – it's about effective communication!

But if you catch yourself prepping your next acidic one-liner instead of truly listening to the discourse, it might be time to stop and take a breath. You've turned a discussion into a duel.

Remember that winning isn't always about landing the hardest punch. Sometimes, it's about knowing when to step out of the ring. There will be moments when a zinger tossed in the middle of a heated dispute can do more harm than good – to your reputation, that is!

There may also be times when getting the last word becomes an imperative if you need, and are determined, to win the argument and you have begun to question the merits of your own case. Then it's time for a withering deflection. This is a strategy beloved by politicians worldwide when cornered into defending a weak point. How do I know? Take it from yours truly; once, or twice, I have found myself navigating that treacherous political battlefield during the four decades of my career. But at least admit to yourself that you have crossed the line between discussing ideas and fighting to win or survive.

While being the person to deliver the final punchline doesn't necessarily mean you're left wearing the crown, there may be times when you opt to slip on that debating armour and deliver your verbal jab with the precision of a fencer. Especially when approached by a bravado-infused, self-loving bulldozer or a contentious know-it-all who actually knows nothing, I say: release the kraken! Employ that well-crafted insult when your kind demeanour is misconstrued as a red-carpet welcome for them to walk over you.

Then comes the tantalising allure of having the last piece of the conversational pie. Delectable, isn't it? Mind you, this isn't a mere power game. It's a nuanced dance, a duel of wits and ripostes. It isn't about unabashed dominance, but eloquence, persuasion, and a knack for pressing that "mute" button on someone's verbal remote at just the right time. Tempted? Turn the pages, and let's dive deep into the warren of this ancient art together.

Our desired destination is not so much to annihilate our opponent, but to encourage communication that enhances our position. Whether you're looking to master the flow and tempo of debates, make sense of heated discussions, or just hone your discursive acuity, this book will arm you with tools to command attention and gracefully sculpt dialogue. There will also be scenarios when your best course is to choose an alternative, non-combative strategy. It will come down to you and what is best, taking account of the circumstances and the likely impact of your response. That's the crux of *Witty Putdowns and Clever Insults*.

Behold the putdown! An enduring symbol of cheeky power, a testament to a sharp mind, a well-loaded linguistic weapon that can drop opponents, sway opinions, solve disputes, or even blare the trumpet of change. Frankly, I don't want to live in a world that is bland, humdrum, and filled with insipid vanilla spokespersons who put their remarks through a linguistic sieve to ensure they serve up a flavourless blend of politically correct freakery and mundane ordinariness. Characters and colour are sadly diminishing in our society as the woke-obsessed movement attempts to squeeze out any descriptive language they haven't sanctioned. As a defender of Freedom of Speech, I will support the right of someone to say what they must, within the framework of the law and the truth. So, I'm all in when it comes to the use of putdowns and witty sarcasm – if the right conditions prevail.

I recognise that, in this society, there are those who seek to restrict what individuals say and how they express themselves. The PC brigade led the charge, but it has now morphed into the *woke* movement.

This metamorphosis began with self-anointed language arbiters policing any and every violation of what they considered to be extreme or offensive terms. This has now reached a level where *Wokies* aggressively and publicly pursue those who do not conform to the standards which are set and daily updated by these supreme *woke* beings.

None of my aversion to 'people cloning' and 'social engineering' lessens my desire to see language practised with thought and decorum. Peppered throughout this publication, you will read cautions about the circumstances, appropriateness, and probative value of striking with an ill-considered and inappropriate jab. This isn't to diminish the usefulness of applying the art, it is to emphasise that there will be instances when the risk outweighs any benefit, and the potential consequences, even if unintended, would be unworthy of you. But more of this as we continue our journey.

Firing this missile takes more than rhetoric – it requires a mixologist's skill for concocting with precision, wit, psychology, understanding, and empathy. We shall attempt to unearth the hidden secrets of wielding words powerfully and watch the transformation they ignite. Together, we'll uncover the delightfully savage art of sallies, and in doing so, leave a lasting impression on everyone we meet, one clever comeback at a time.

Spectator reaction is the most potent aspect of measuring the value of a putdown, and your audience won't have a uniform sense of humour, nor will they necessarily have the same tolerance for personal barbs. Obviously, they may not be as intelligent as you – so be careful. As an example:

 "If you were any more inbred, you'd be a sandwich."

This putdown fired quickly will shock and probably horrify most of your audience – they will only hear an offensive insult. It still weighs heavily on the abuse scale, but the smarter listener might pick up the deft twin implication of "inbred" and "in bread" and have a chuckle. If the person against whom it is directed has been obnoxious and everyone is fed-up with them, your audience will likely be more sympathetic. To some degree, it will depend on how and against whom you render the line, whether anyone in the room will speak to you afterwards. Timing and delivery are important elements of a memorable putdown. As comedian Frank Carson would have said:

 "It's the way I tell 'em."

Let's lay out my full confession. Although I'm playing preacher now, I wasn't always so choirboy-like with my words. In my political career, I carved my path during challenging years, often with all the subtleness of a sledgehammer. But in calmer seas, I can appreciate the power of the well-timed clever strike, rather than unleashing a tempest of insults at an adversary – a switch, my rancorous and ungenerous political opponents might claim, I conveniently didn't flick until I was making my way out the door.

It is true that I might, just occasionally, have been a rule-bender in the gladiatorial arena of politics. I spent my apprenticeship years trading verbal fire and brimstone against a turbulent historic backdrop where the linguistic hammers fell heavily and hard. However, I modestly boast that I aged like a fine political wine and now prefer the zesty appeal of a witty snap to verbally pummelling foes with brass knuckles.... most of the time.

Sure, all the namby-pamby talk about "respectful communication", "fostering healthy relationships", and "finding shared interests" is all well and good. But realistically, sometimes the entry is a cul-de-sac with no means of escape, other than introducing your rival to a length of untreated lumber – verbally, of course. No more is this true than when under fire and faced with fashioning a retaliatory witty comeback. Actress Ilka Chase found herself the subject of faint praise from Humphrey Bogart:

Bogart: *"I enjoyed your book. Who wrote it for you?"*

Chase: *"Darling, I'm so glad you liked it. Who read it to you?"*

Had he been inclined or adept at continuing the repartee, he might have lobbed a further shot over the net:

"You're right, of course. Someone must have read it to me. I would never have purchased a copy."

But then I doubt Ilka would have been left gasping. Her return barb could well have finished the rally with a brutal forehand smash.

There will be some who will view participating in this sport with as much fondness as I do operating a supermarket self-checkout. To them, I say, you've bought the wrong book. Don't complain. Don't send me an anonymous message. As Yogi Berra opined:

"I never answer anonymous letters."

And look, I get it. Everybody prefers the idea of conflict-free, positive chats. But how often does that genuinely happen? In an ideal world, we'd always be cruising on the highway of respectful dialogue. Unfortunately, now and again, there will be detours, and the scenic route will turn into the rocky road of friction. Sometimes, surprisingly, people just don't seem to get the fact that you're always right. That's when the putdown toolbox kicks in. A well-crafted wisecrack, used sparingly and delivered with precision, could be just the ticket to getting back on the smooth path. So, if the banter fails and the shared interests are as few as hens' teeth, this book will equip you with the tools needed for an elegantly executed verbal backhand. I'll serve first, shall I?

Insults come in many guises; to your face, behind your back, graffitied on walls, anonymously, online, via the means of grunting or rude gestures, mockingly pretending to fall asleep while you're talking, eye-rolling, in song and poetry and in every other conceivable method of communication. Most of us have done one or some, so don't be so self-righteous. Remember seeing a classmate with a note stuck on his back –

"Kick me hard – I deserve it." Or on the back of the fattest child in the class – "Follow me to McDonald's". Par for the course when I was young, but do it today and you will experience a few days off school for bullying. Which raises another consideration – putdowns must be judged in the context and convention of the age in which they're used.

Insults are formed against many target pedigrees. Individuals are by far the most likely victims, though nations and groups of all hues have been picked on and picked apart. Even inanimate objects can be satirised. Think of the inoffensive alphabet – who could speak disparagingly about a poor letter doing its best to help mankind to communicate? Well! Shakespeare in King Lear did it with relish:

 "Thou whoreson zed! Thou unnecessary letter!"

He clearly never had a Zen moment or zigzagged across a field. While it can be dangerous to follow the Latin example of dropping the good old *zed,* I shall, nonetheless, to appease the erudite followers of the bard, try hard to cover the A to Y of putdowns in the pages that follow.

* * *

POLITICAL PUTDOWNS

S harpen those claws as we raise the curtain on a world where political and historic figures alike engage in combat, not with swords and shields, but with biting repartee and sassy snaps, in the savage, yet sometimes humorous field of political putdowns.

Many imagine the landscape of politics as an arid desert marked by sterile facts, monotonous speeches, and bland recitations of governance and law. But nothing could be further from the truth! Peel back the constitutional canvas, and you'll discover a vibrant jungle of quips, jests, and the most delicious of insults, flung in the faces of adversaries, creating, or destroying legends with a wag of the tongue.

This is a captivating realm where language serves as a sharp sword and wit reigns supreme. It's the world of verbal warfare, where the pen is mightier than the sword, but the tongue — oh, the tongue — can pierce the armour of egos and deflate the pompous.

In this chapter and others, I've compiled a collection of remarkable soundbites from the finest performers of this dark art. However, towards the end of many chapters, you'll find numerous excerpts from a legion of other individuals worth studying.

The story is told that Richard Sheridan, a Liberal MP was walking through London when he was sandwiched between two Tory Peers.

Attempting to intimidate him, the most outspoken mocked:

> *"I say Sherry, we were just discussing whether you were a rogue or a fool."*

Sheridan replied:

> *"Why, I do believe I am between both."*

Clarence Darrow, an American lawyer, showed more than a measure of scepticism about politicians:

> *"When I was a boy I was told that anybody could become President; I'm beginning to believe it."*

Invective is part of both the British and American political tradition and who can overlook Winston Churchill, the putdown grandmaster? Whether you found him charming or sardonic, he had a droll way to deflate haughty egos without even a hint of malice. Case in point:

> British MP Bessie Braddock: *"You are drunk."*
>
> Churchill, without missing a beat: *"And you, Bessie, are ugly. But I shall be sober in the morning."*

Ouch! A double dose of Churchillian irony, served ice-cold, without a sprinkle of remorse.

Another celebrated sample of his skill was demonstrated when he responded to Lady Astor, the first woman to sit in the British Parliament.

> Lady Astor: *"Sir, if you were my husband, I would poison your tea,"*
>
> Churchill: *"Madam, if I were your husband, I would drink it."*

This exchange showcased not only Churchill's quick thinking, but also his ability to turn the tables on his opponents through sharp humour. However, he didn't always get his own way with Lady Astor:

> Churchill: *"I venture to say that my Rt Hon friend, so redolent of other knowledge, knows nothing of farming. I'll even make a bet that she doesn't know how many toes a pig has."*

Lady Astor: *"Oh, yes, I do. Take off your little shoosies and we'll count them together."*

Another historic zinger features Thomas Reed, one-time U.S. House of Representatives Speaker. When asked whether he'd heard that his enemy, fellow politician Roscoe Conkling, was due to become an ambassador, Reed replied:

"I cannot imagine any country to which he could be sent where he would not do incalculable mischief."

A simple sentence, neatly drilled between the ribs.

Churchill was rightly critical of the weakness of the then British Prime Minister, Neville Chamberlain, and often fired cutting remarks in his direction.

"At the depths of that dusty soul there is nothing but abject surrender".

— WINSTON CHURCHILL, PM

Then mockingly added:

"An appeaser is one who feeds a crocodile hoping it will eat him last"

— WINSTON CHURCHILL, PM

Spain's former prime minister, José María Aznar, savoured the good old "your mum" putdown. In response to an opponent's jibe at his lack of a higher educational degree, Aznar shot back:

"I only hold one degree, the same one as your mother, from the School of Life."

It's hard for an adversary to come back with a response that doesn't also insult mum. Being rude about mums doesn't poll well.

Former US Vice President, Hubert Humphrey, held a less than charitable position about the views of others:

> *"The right to be heard does not automatically include the right to be taken seriously."*

Former British Prime Minister Margaret Thatcher, engaged in formidable putdowns. One was directed at a fellow Conservative Party member, who disagreed with her policies. Thatcher quipped:

> *"I am extraordinarily patient, provided I get my own way in the end."*

This remark perfectly encapsulated her steadfastness and determination, while also subtly asserting her authority within her party.

In the realm of U.S. politics, one cannot overlook the biting wit of former President Ronald Reagan. Reagan has long been a favourite of mine at both putdowns and using humorous stories as message parables. He was a master of delivering memorable, humorous jabs at his opponents. During a 1984 debate, he faced off against his Democratic challenger, Walter Mondale. Mondale had been questioning Reagan's age and ability to govern, and the President deftly deflected the critique, saying,

> *"I will not exploit, for political purposes, my opponent's youth and inexperience."*

This quip not only changed the atmosphere, but also indicated that, far from being too old, he had a sharp mind as well as being a charismatic leader.

Then up pops the undisguised disparaging insult – they can be very telling, especially in the cut and thrust of exchanges. Take Sarah Palin's reference to Joe Biden during the 2008 U.S. vice-presidential debate:

> *"I've met smarter sandwiches."*

But the art of the political putdown isn't limited to the debating stage. In the age of social media, politicians have found new arenas to engage in verbal sparring. Enter Donald Trump, the implacable wielder of Twitter (now X) insults. With clever wordplay and relentless nicknames, he has spun his web of putdowns, leaving opponents flustered and followers entertained. Love him or loathe him, you can't ignore him, nor his unique flair for caustic commentary. Trump's putdowns have become a signature part of his political persona. Most amount to humorous, though sometimes biting, name calling of opponents. Crooked Hilary (Hillary Clinton), Sloppy Steve (Steve Bannon), Crazy Bernie (Sen. Bernie Sanders), Jeff Flakey (Sen. Jeff Flake), Pocahontas (Sen. Elizabeth Warren, who claims Native American ancestry) and Al Frankenstein (Al Franken) form the tip of the spear, but are just a small part of what is likely to be an ever-expanding catalogue, which demonstrates the relaxed nature of US libel laws.

The disparaging nicknames are not confined to domestic opponents – and at times former friends – they include international leaders. The Syrian President Bashar al-Assad became "Animal Assad", leading Saudis were accused of 'milking' their country for years and a former British Ambassador was summed up as "wacky, a very stupid guy". Brussels, he described as "a hell hole", Germany as "very delinquent" and China – "that caused the Covid pandemic" or "Kung Flu" as *The Donald* put it, were accused of "rip offs" and "rampant theft".

Oral knockaboutary is a time-honoured tradition and captivating aspect of politics that showcases wit, intelligence, and the ability to think on one's feet. Whether it's Winston Churchill's acerbic quips, Reagan's quick retorts, or the modern era's social media takedowns, these well-crafted and often entertaining remarks have the power to shape narratives and leave lasting impressions. They serve to entertain audiences, bolster a politician's image, and sometimes even sway public opinion. The craft isn't just an heirloom from history, it is more widely and fiercely performed today and, if I am to judge, it will grow exponentially in the future.

Yet, it's not always the politician who engages in verbal savagery. Look at this killer question in 1988 from Bernard Shaw of CNN to Michael Dukakis, a lifelong adversary of the Death penalty:

 Shaw: *"If Kitty Dukakis were raped and murdered, would you favour an irrevocable death penalty for the killer?"*

Dukakis: *"No, I don't, and I think you know I have opposed the death penalty all my life. I don't see any evidence it is a deterrent."*

It became a turning point in the election. Not because of the content of his response, but because of its lack of passion and his failure to display those natural feelings anyone would have in the imagined circumstances. It goes to the heart of practising verbal swordplay. Dukakis came across as a politically correct technocrat, out of touch with everyday people's emotions.

When you appear on the public stage, you don't speak with words alone. The public take in your appearance, your expressions, your emotions, and yes, your affinity, sympathy, and awareness of the natural human perspective of what you are saying.

There are occasions when the material for a putdown just falls into your lap. I recall a tough meeting in Parliament Buildings in Belfast with Prime Minister Tony Blair. I had serious doubts about the candour and accuracy of the line, about which he was trying to convince my colleagues and me. He must have observed that scepticism from my facial expression, but just as I was about to interrupt to express my disbelief, the building's fire alarm rang out at an exceedingly high decibel level. The PM immediately stopped the conversation, and, addressing nobody specifically, asked:

Blair: *"What's that noise?"*

Me: *"It's the lie detector, Prime Minister."*

Woodrow Wilson was governor of New Jersey, when he was informed that one of the state's senators had died and it was his duty to appoint a replacement. A local politician, who couldn't wait to make a bid for the post called the Governor, even before the poor deceased senator had been laid to rest, and said,

"I'd like to take the senator's place."

Woodrow Wilson replied:

"It's okay with me, if it's okay with the undertaker."

Now that's a conversation stopper!

A lack of thought in a debate can translate the orator into a victim of his own careless language choices:

Lord Chatham: *"If I cannot speak standing, I will speak sitting; and if I cannot speak sitting, I will speak lying."*

Lord North: *"Which he will do in whatever position he speaks."*

Attacking an opponent because he is more youthful or less experienced is often used to elevate the politician who has more time served. Perhaps it was best addressed by businessman Ross Perot in a presidential debate. He did not even wait for the accusation to be levelled at him:

 Perot: *"I don't have any experience in running up a 4-trillion-dollar debt, I don't have any experience in gridlock government where nobody takes responsibility for anything, and everybody blames everybody else."*

When, in 1940, Thomas E. Dewey announced his candidacy for president, he faced an early onslaught. He was 38 years old but, by the measure of those days, deemed too young and inexperienced by his opponents:

 "Dewey has tossed his diaper into the ring."

— HAROLD L. ICKES (ROOSEVELT'S COLLEAGUE)

After a Dewey speech, Ickes returned to the theme:

 "I did not listen because I have a baby of my own."

Herbert Hoover, the 31st US President, was travelling on the slip road to the Great Depression, when he shared his concerns with President Calvin Coolidge, his predecessor in office, about the lack of improvement his rescue measures were having on the weakening and slowing American economy.

 "You can't expect to see calves running in the field the day after you put the bull to the cows."

— PRESIDENT COOLIDGE

 "No, but I would at least like to see some contented cows."

— PRESIDENT HOOVER

The talent of putdowns ranges from pouring scorn to unfiltered abuse and every sneering ratchet in between. Some of my favourites include:

> "Mr Depew says that if you open my mouth and drop in a dinner, up will come a speech. But I warn you that if you open up your mouths and drop in one of Mr Depew's speeches, up will come your dinner."
>
> — JOSEPH CHOATE

> "He's so dumb, he thinks Cheerios are doughnut seeds."
>
> — JIM HIGHTOWER ON DAN QUAYLE

> "The cocks may crow, but it's the hen that lays the egg,"
>
> — MARGARET THATCHER

> "He's the life and soul of the party. But he's not the man you want driving you home at the end of the evening."
>
> — AMBER RUDD ABOUT BORIS JOHNSON

> "He can't see a belt without hitting below it."
>
> — MARGOT ASQUITH ABOUT LLOYD GEORGE

> "I remember, when I was a child, being taken to the celebrated Barnum's Circus, which contained an exhibition of freaks and monstrosities; but the exhibit on the programme which I most desired to see was the one described as 'The Boneless Wonder'. My parents judged that the spectacle would be too revolting and demoralising for my youthful eyes, and I have waited fifty years to see The Boneless Wonder sitting on the Treasury Bench."
>
> — WINSTON CHURCHILL ON RAMSEY MACDONALD

> "St Patrick's Day is the day when anybody who is anybody leaves the island of Ireland to celebrate our patron saint 3,000 miles away in America. You couldn't make it up."
>
> — RT HON ARLENE FOSTER, FORMER FIRST MINISTER OF NORTHERN IRELAND AND NOW BARONESS FOSTER OF AGHADRUMSEE

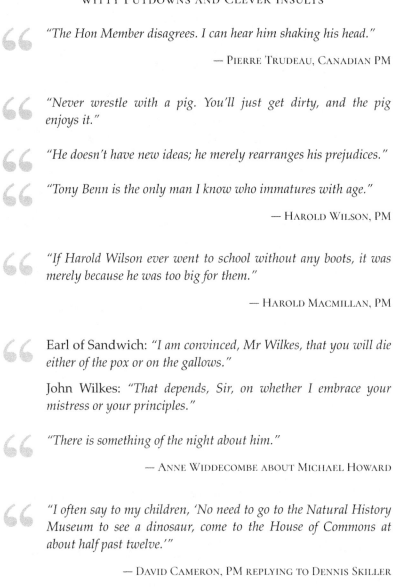

"The Hon Member disagrees. I can hear him shaking his head."

— PIERRE TRUDEAU, CANADIAN PM

"Never wrestle with a pig. You'll just get dirty, and the pig enjoys it."

"He doesn't have new ideas; he merely rearranges his prejudices."

"Tony Benn is the only man I know who immatures with age."

— HAROLD WILSON, PM

"If Harold Wilson ever went to school without any boots, it was merely because he was too big for them."

— HAROLD MACMILLAN, PM

Earl of Sandwich: *"I am convinced, Mr Wilkes, that you will die either of the pox or on the gallows."*

John Wilkes: *"That depends, Sir, on whether I embrace your mistress or your principles."*

"There is something of the night about him."

— ANNE WIDDECOMBE ABOUT MICHAEL HOWARD

"I often say to my children, 'No need to go to the Natural History Museum to see a dinosaur, come to the House of Commons at about half past twelve.'"

— DAVID CAMERON, PM REPLYING TO DENNIS SKILLER

"If a million people believe a foolish thing, it is still a foolish thing."

> *"He's a mixture of Harry Houdini and a greased piglet. He is barely human in his elusiveness. Nailing Blair is like trying to pin jelly to a wall."*
>
> — BORIS JOHNSON, PM ON TONY BLAIR, PM

> *"When Edwina Currie goes to the dentist, he needs the anaesthetic."*
>
> — FRANK DOBSON MP ON TORY MINISTER EDWINA CURRIE

> Member: *"On a Point of Order! Is the Honourable Member allowed to act the eejit (idiot)?"*
>
> The Speaker: *"He is not acting."*

> *"The House has noticed the Prime Minister's (Gordon Brown) remarkable transformation in the last few weeks from Stalin to Mr Bean."*
>
> — VINCE CABLE MP, LIB DEM LEADER

> *"Too bad all the people who know how to run the country are busy driving cabs and cutting hair."*
>
> — GEORGE BURNS, COMEDIAN

> *"Greater love hath no man than this, that he lay down his friends for his life."*
>
> — JEREMY THORPE LIBERAL MP ON MACMILLAN'S 'NIGHT OF THE LONG KNIVES' CABINET RESHUFFLE

> *"If the word 'No' was removed from the English language, Ian Paisley would be speechless."*
>
> — JOHN HUME MP, THEN LEADER OF THE SDLP

In 1992 Dan Quayle boasted that he intended to be "a pit bull" in the upcoming campaign against the Democratic presidential candidate Bill

Clinton and his running mate Al Gore. When Clinton was asked for his reaction, he joked:

 "That's got every fire hydrant in America worried."

— PRESIDENT BILL CLINTON

My long-time friend and colleague, Sammy Wilson MP, has always been good at finding the humour in any situation and is a popular performer at Party Conferences. At one of our annual get-togethers, he came holding a Dublin-published magazine with a front cover shared between its two main stories. One was adorned with a photo of former IRA leader Gerry Adams and the other with an attractive girl who, the magazine informed its readers, was "the new face of *Wonderbra*". Sammy calculated:

 "I'm certain he has been lifted more often and with greater necessity than she has."

The same magazine divulged that Adams was a keen environmentalist and spent time communing with the fruits of nature.

 Sammy Wilson: *"I read that Gerry Adams talks to flowers and hugs trees. Yes, he's a tree hugger. I suppose we shouldn't be surprised, given how often he has been handled by the Special Branch."*

In another life, Sammy was the Head of Economics at an East Belfast School. I appointed him as Finance Minister when I became First Minister. He had a solid grip on the detail of the department's policies and activities and was always relaxed when answering questions in the Assembly, until he responded to Green Party leader Steven Agnew:

 Sammy Wilson: *"If the Member did a wee bit of economics first, he would not ask such a stupid question."*

Steven Agnew: *"Well, you taught me."*

Navigating the turbulent seas of politics requires unprecedented dexterity in both wording and action. Politicians are constantly scrutinised – each word they emit is dissected and spun within the relentless mill of public opinion. One might then ask why, given such meticulous scrutiny, would politicians resort to putdowns and insults?

Of course, not all politicians indulge in the art and can still reach the top. One of my successors as party leader, Sir Jeffrey Donaldson, possessed that calm equilibrium that seldom savages but consistently seeks to conquer through reason. Such personalities when provoked to react outside their customary manner often demand more attention. The government, some decades ago, had laboured for many months to produce a *Framework Document* which was to be the blueprint for negotiations. So incensed was Jeffrey by its content that he ripped it in two, at a press conference, and tossed it aside. I suspect the authors were insulted but he had made his point.

Taking into account the inherent risks, would the potential negative repercussions not outweigh the precarious satisfaction of a well-lobbed barb? Weighing the potential risks and rewards of this approach should encourage politicians to think hard before striking out with verbal jabs on a stage where public opinion is merciless. Yet, soundbites and drama rule the day, they're an instrument of dominance, a well-aimed insult can become a prism through which the masses judge a leader's wit and intelligence. It's a path to popularity and can destabilise an opponent, eliciting reactive emotions that may manifest as flustered responses or defensive behaviour. The ability to unsettle an opponent in this way can be perceived as a display of control, authority, and tactical superiority.

But one wrong step, and the crowd turns against you, branding you mean-spirited or a bully, though in the heat of the brawl, it can be hard to apply the brakes. In this game of verbal jousting, the victor may be the spectator, left amused, aghast, or both.

For every politician that boosts their appeal through wit and cunning, there's another who stumbles. In this verbal skirmish, a failed or harshly uncouth insult can hurt a politician's standing, making them appear mean-spirited and turning public opinion against them.

Famously, during the 1988 U.S. Vice Presidential debate, Senator Lloyd Bentsen's response to Dan Quayle, who sought to liken himself to JFK, was:

> *"Senator, I served with Jack Kennedy. I knew Jack Kennedy. Jack Kennedy was a friend of mine. Senator, you're no Jack Kennedy."*

This is considered a classic, damaging Quayle's campaign, while boosting Bentsen's prestige.

In 2016, Senator Marco Rubio's attempt to hit back at President Donald Trump, who had referred to the Senator as "Little Rubio", left him badly bruised. Rubio admitted that Trump was indeed taller than him but added that Trump had small hands for his height:

 "And you know what they say about guys with small hands."

The crowd was stunned. Rubio, realising his gaff. then added,

 "You can't trust them."

But it was too late. Not knowing when to stop digging, Rubio targeted Trump's famous "tan", stating:

 " ... he doesn't sweat, because his pores are clogged from the spray tan. Donald Trump isn't gonna make America great, he's gonna make America orange."

Rubio's remarks were then seen as off brand and contributed to doubts about his dependability. Today, he might get away with it, for the passage of time seems to raise the acceptability levels, and jibes targeted at someone who constantly performs the art themselves are regarded as fair game.

President Donald Trump has never held back on criticism of the media. For the most part, he comes out swinging and often lands a fierce blow. Now and again someone from outside the ring jumps in and catches him on the chin.

 "Nothing funny about tired Saturday Night Live on Fake News NBC! How do the Networks get away with these total Republican hit jobs without retribution?"

— PRESIDENT DONALD TRUMP

 "One thing that makes America great is that the people can laugh at you without retribution."

— DEMOCRATIC CONGRESSMAN TED LIEU RESPONDED

The Donald Trump v Hillary Clinton debates produced their moments when horns were locked. Trump argued that he had the temperament to be President but Clinton did not. This sparked a fiery exchange:

> *"It's just awfully good that someone with the temperament of Donald Trump is not in charge of the laws in the country."*

— Hillary Clinton

> *"Because you'd be in jail."*

— Donald Trump

Just as TV debates can produce some great material for the avid putdown collector, so too can interventions and disturbances during campaign stump speeches.

William Howard Taff, the 27th US President was on the campaign trail when an over-enthusiastic heckler threw a cabbage at him. Taft immediately stopped speaking, dramatically starred at the cabbage at his feet and responded:

> *"Ladies and Gentlemen, I see that one of my opponents has lost his head."*

Politicians also need to remember their audience will be diverse; a jab that one person finds hilarious, another may deem derogatory. The divisive nature of humour can polarise the crowd, cementing the support of existing followers, while antagonising potential supporters.

Essentially, putdowns in politics are high-risk – high-reward manoeuvres, a dance along the knife's edge. When executed with aplomb, they bolster reputations and command respect and admiration. However, a lapse of tact or an overtly aggressive slur can corrode public support and shatter carefully constructed political personas. The question then isn't whether putdowns aid or harm politicians, but how adept politicians are in their construction and delivery.

While most insults contained in this publication are one-liners, that need not always be the case; nor do they need to contain humour. Having a clever answer to a serious attack may require a lengthier rejoinder. Here is an example from my own life and times.

The setting is the Chamber of the Northern Ireland Assembly, and I am at the Despatch Box, responding to members' comments at the end of a debate. The motion being discussed touched on how to deal with our country's divided past. I am leading a power-sharing government, comprising ancient foes now working together. Not everyone has come to terms with the new epoch, including some within my unionist tradition, whose voice in the Assembly is the leader of a small party antipathetic to the new arrangements. He has, during the debate, launched another attack on my party's relationship with former foes and again criticised our participation in the new political dispensation. I respond:

"As I look across the Chamber, the picture that comes into my mind is that of a certain Japanese man. That isn't a racist comment, nor is it any reference to the appearance of the Member for North Antrim. I think the man's name was Hiroo Onoda. He was sent to a Philippine island during the Second World War to carry out disruptive acts, with the aim of hindering the allies should they seek to use the island as an operational base. However, he stayed in the jungle long after V-E Day, believing messages sent to him that the war was over was an enemy hoax. Although men went around the island with loudspeakers to tell him that the war was over, he hid and simply would not believe it. Though they dropped leaflets on the island, pleading with him to come home as the conflict had ended, he still would not believe it. Twenty-nine years after the war, he came out.

It seems to me that the Member for North Antrim still has not come to terms with the fact that in Northern Ireland we have left behind the era in which he seems to be content to mire himself. This is a new age – we are trying to move forward."

The purpose, at the time, of telling the story was never to convince the Member, nor indeed to put him down. Rather, it was to demonstrate that, far from embodying a Samurai spirit, he, and those who thought like him, were prisoners of their refusal to accept a new reality. Being in denial was thereby cheating others of the opportunity to make real and positive progress.

In navigating the breadth of political putdowns, special attention has to be given to the Australian Parliament. It can be a biker-bar roughhouse and there is no immunity for politicians inside or outside either – certainly not when the sharp-tongued PM Paul Keating was about. I think he deserves his own section – though it's not for the squeamish.

> Keating: *"The Leader of the Opposition is more to be pitied than despised, the poor old thing. The Liberal Party of Australia ought to put him down like a faithful old dog because he is of no use to it and of no use to the nation."*

> Keating: *"He's wound up like a thousand-day clock! One more half-turn and there'll be springs and sprockets all over the building. Mr Speaker, give him a Valium."*

> Keating: *"You were heard in silence, so some of you scumbags on the front bench should just wait a minute until you hear the responses from me."*

> Keating: *"The Opposition could not manage a tart shop."*

> Keating: *"Oh, look,... the little desiccated coconut's under pressure and he's attacking anything he can get his hands on."*

> Keating: *"You boxhead! You wouldn't know. You are flat out counting past 10, you stupid, foul-mouthed grub."*

> Keating: *"Whether the Treasurer wished to go there or not – I would forbid him going to the Senate to account to (that) unrepresentative swill."*

> Keating: *"I am not like the Leader of the Opposition. I did not slither out of the Cabinet room like a mangy maggot."*

> Keating: *"It was the limpest performance I have ever seen. It was like being flogged with a warm lettuce."*

> Keating (to protesters haranguing him): *"Go and get a job! Go and do a bit of work like the rest of us."*

> Keating: *"He is simply a shiver looking for a spine to run up."*

> *"What we have got is a dead carcass, swinging in the breeze, but nobody will cut it down to replace him."*

> — KEATING ON JOHN HOWARD

> *"I suppose that the Honourable Gentleman's hair, like his intellect, will recede into the darkness."*

> — KEATING ON ANDREW PEACOCK

> *"We're not interested in the views of painted, perfumed gigolos."*

> — KEATING ON ANDREW PEACOCK

> *"You remind me of the guy who fell off a skyscraper. As he passed each floor, he kept saying, 'So far, so good'."*

> — KEATING ON JOHN HEWSON

> *"He's a low-calibre man firing blanks."*

> — KEATING ON ALEXANDER DOWNER

> Hewson: *"If you're so confident, why won't you call an election?"*

Keating: *"Because I want to do you slowly."*

I'd think twice before accepting an invitation to his barbie.

Perhaps U.S. writer Paul Theroux was not far from the mark when he judged:

> *"The Australian Book of Etiquette is a very slim volume."*

It tempts me to make another visit.

And so, as we gingerly tiptoe onward through the minefield of political insults, we're reminded that humour is indeed a true democratising force – ripping into facades, humanising the grand stages, and breathing life into the faded headlines. At their best, "cutting words" are not merely insults slung in the face of the opponent, but comedic gems, pieces of performance-art, requiring timing, wit, intellect, and a daring disregard for personal consequence.

Whether you're a statesperson or an everyday guy or gal, such repartee can become veritable tools of power or destruction, agents of connection or discord. Whatever we may think about the art of political satire, it is here to stay. It is the Shakespearean theatre of the modern world, where history, comedy, and cringeworthy blunders blend into a potent cocktail. To laugh or not to laugh? That is the question.

THE 'OOPS!' MOMENT

This chapter, for the most part, has up to now considered the language of politicians who insulted others or were insulted by others. Yet, just occasionally, we chance upon a politician who shoots himself in the foot by saying exactly what he thinks about the electorate, whether he intended it to be recorded or not. In the intentional column, we find the 3rd Marquess of Salisbury and former UK Prime Minister, Robert Gascoyne, who, more than a century ago, gave us his take on electioneering and voters.

 "The days and weeks of screwed-up smiles and laboured courtesy, the mock geniality, the hearty shake of the filthy hand, the chuckling reply that must be made to the coarse joke, the loathsome, choking compliment that must be paid to the grimy wife and sluttish daughter, the indispensable flattery of the vilest religious prejudices, the wholesale deglutition of hypocritical pledges."

I don't think that such a comment would pass without a righteous hysterical media storm today. It is neither a good look for a politician, nor does it suggest respect for the democratic process and, even more importantly, for the people who elect governments – and fire them.

Even Sir Winston Churchill exhibited a lack of respect for the voting public:

 "The best argument against democracy is a five-minute conversation with the average voter."

From the unintentional column comes a more modern example of a politician being caught out. During the British General Election of 2010, we witnessed a 'hot mic' moment at the conclusion of PM Gordon Brown's tour of Rochdale with a TV crew who wired him up for sound. Mr Brown was challenged by a lady whom his staff had cleared as she was a party supporter. Her comments about the economy and immigration were off-message. As the PM was being driven away, not aware that his microphone was still on, he said:

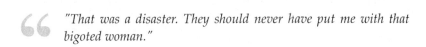

> *"That was a disaster. They should never have put me with that bigoted woman."*

Poor Gordon suffered headline news criticism and eventually had to return to Rochdale with his tail between his legs to apologise to the "bigoted woman".

A COLLECTION OF POLITICAL ZINGERS

> *"In politics, stupidity is not a handicap."*
>
> — NAPOLEON BONAPARTE

> *"He has all the virtues I dislike and none of the vices I admire."*
>
> — WINSTON CHURCHILL, PM

> "He has the mind of a pig and the soul of a sewer."
>
> — PRESIDENT HARRY S. TRUMAN

> *"His ignorance is encyclopaedic."*
>
> — ABBA EVAN ON MENACHEM BEGIN

> *"His problem is that he lacks the power of conversation but not the power of speech."*
>
> — MARGARET THATCHER, PM

> *"He can't tell the difference between a grand gesture and an empty platitude."*
>
> — President Barack Obama

> *"He has the ability to speak six languages, but can't say 'no' in any of them."*
>
> — Margaret Thatcher, PM

> *"He's like a one-man circus, always juggling the truth."*
>
> — President Bill Clinton

> *"He has the inspirational qualities of a damp rag and the appearance of a low-grade bank clerk."*
>
> — Nigel Farage on the President of the European Council

> *"He's a man of firm convictions – except in the face of reality."*
>
> — President George H. W. Bush

> *"His speeches are like bulls – they look better from a distance."*
>
> — Winston Churchill PM

> *"He has a mind like a steel trap – rusted shut."*
>
> — Elizabeth Warren

> *"He has the mind of a serial killer."*
>
> — Boris Johnson PM on Jeremy Corbyn

> *"He has all the characteristics of a dog – except loyalty."*
>
> — Sam Houston on Mirabeau Bonaparte Lamar

"His finest hour lasted a minute and a half."

— MARGARET THATCHER PM ON MICHAEL HESELTINE

"He is a self-made man and worships his creator."

— JOHN BRIGHT ON BENJAMIN DISRAELI, PM

"His brains could revolve inside a peanut shell without touching the sides."

— ANEURIN BEVAN ON SIR ALEC DOUGLAS-HOME

"If you put his brain on the edge of a razor blade, it would look like a BB (Mini box car) rolling down a four-lane highway."

— FRANK MANKIEWICZ ON DAN QUAYLE

"He's like a dead fish on the end of a line, not even wriggling."

— DAVID LLOYD GEORGE, PM ON NEVILLE CHAMBERLAIN, PM

"An empty taxi pulled up and Clement Attlee got out."

— ATTRIBUTED TO WINSTON CHURCHILL, PM

"He can't help it; he was born with a silver foot in his mouth."

— ANN RICHARDS, REFERRING TO PRESIDENT GEORGE H. W. BUSH

"He occasionally stumbled over the truth, but hastily got up and hurried on as if nothing had happened."

— WINSTON CHURCHILL, PM

"His mind is so open that ideas simply pass through it."

— CLIFFORD ODETS

"The trouble with our liberal friends is not that they're ignorant; it's just that they know so much that isn't so."

— President Ronald Regan

"Being powerful is like being a lady. If you have to tell people you are, you aren't."

— Margaret Thatcher, PM

"I don't think George Bush is a bad guy. I just think he's in way over his head."

— President Joe Biden

"His speeches leave one with the impression of an army of pompous phrases moving over the landscape in search of an idea."

— President Franklin D. Roosevelt on Herbert Hoover

"You have sat too long for any good you have been doing. In the name of God, go!"

— Oliver Cromwell, addressing the Rump Parliament

"He has more in his mouth than in his mind."

— Queen Elizabeth I on Sir Walter Raleigh

"He inherited some good instincts from his Quaker forebears, but by diligent hard work, he overcame them."

— James Reston on President Richard Nixon

"All the world wondered as they waited, ... and waited, ... and waited."

— Sen John McCain on President Bill Clinton's hesitancy

"He's the kind of man who picks your pocket, steals your watch, and tells you the time while he's doing it."

"He's the only man I know who can strut sitting down."

— FORMER CANADIAN PM, JOHN DIEFENBAKER

"His mind is less an open book than an open sewer."

— ROY JENKINS MP

"He can compress the most words into the smallest ideas of any man I ever met."

— PRESIDENT ABRAHAM LINCOLN

"He is a man of splendid abilities but utterly corrupt. He shines and stinks like rotten mackerel in the moonlight."

— JOHN RANDOLPH

"His speeches leave long-lasting footprints. Unfortunately, they lead nowhere."

— PRESIDENT GEORGE W. BUSH

"He is a man of great virtue but questionable judgement."

— PRESIDENT JOHN ADAMS

"He could never be mistaken for a man of principle; his entire personality is an apology for one."

— PRESIDENT JOHN F. KENNEDY

"He is the kind of politician who would cut down a redwood tree and then mount the stump to make a speech for conservation."

— ADLAI STEVENSON

"He could argue either side of a case and still lose."

— FORMER SENATOR BARRY GOLDWATER

"He is living proof that man can live without a backbone, but not without a cranium."

— PRESIDENT FRANKLIN D. ROOSEVELT

"He could convince a fish to drown itself."

— BENJAMIN DISRAELI, PM

"He will go down in history like a fizzled-out firecracker."

— MAHATMA GANDHI

"He is a master of the condescending smirk."

— FORMER GERMAN CHANCELLOR ANGELA MERKEL

"He is a triple-headed political enigma: he still thinks in slogans, he talks in clichés, and he acts in confusion."

— ANEURIN BEVAN

"If you ever tell everything you know, you'll still be three-fifths short."

— WALTER MONDALE TO A TALKATIVE POLITICIAN

"He's a triple-breasted man; he'll keep changing his position."

— PRESIDENT RICHARD NIXON

"A politician needs the ability to foretell what is going to happen tomorrow, next week, next month, and next year. And to have the ability afterwards to explain why it didn't happen."

— WINSTON CHURCHILL, PM

"He's too small game to shoot twice."

— President Theodore Roosevelt

"The Senators of the United States have no use for their heads, except to serve as a knot to keep their bodies from unravelling."

— President Woodrow Wilson

"He's a nice guy, but he played too much football with his helmet off."

— President Lyndon B. Johnson on President Gerald Ford

"I wouldn't say she is open-minded on the Middle East so much as empty-headed. She probably thinks Sinai is the plural of sinus."

— Jonathan Aitken MP on Margaret Thatcher, PM

"She's got dyed blonde hair and pouty lips, and a steely blue stare, like a sadistic nurse in a mental hospital."

— Boris Johnson, PM on President Hillary Clinton

"A mutton-headed old mugwump."

— Boris Johnson, PM on Labour Leader Jeremy Corbyn

"In a recent fire, Bob Dole's library burned down. Both books were lost. And he hadn't even finished colouring one of them."

— Jack Kemp, Congressman

"The difference between a misfortune and a calamity is this: If Gladstone fell into the Thames, that would be a misfortune. If anybody pulled him out, that, I suppose, would be a calamity."

— Benjamin Disraeli, PM on Prime Minister William E. Gladstone

"Never confuse sitting on your side with being on your side."

— LORD BANNSIDE, THEN IAN PAISLEY MP

"Half the members of the opposition are not crooks."

— MULTIPLE CLAIMS OF OWNERSHIP

"Attila the Hen."

— SIR CLEMENT FREUD REFERRING TO MARGARET THATCHER, PM

"She is clearly the best man among them."

— BARBARA CASTLE MP ON MARGARET THATCHER, PM

"I am thoroughly in favour of Mrs Thatcher's visit to the Falklands. I find a bit of hesitation, though, about her coming back."

— JOHN MORTIMER, PLAYWRIGHT

"Jezebel."

— LORD BANNSIDE, THEN IAN PAISLEY MP

"I've never killed a man, but I've read many an obituary with great pleasure."

— CLARENCE DARROW

"Always be sincere, even if you don't mean it."

— HARRY S. TRUMAN, PRESIDENT

"Any American who is prepared to run for President should automatically, by definition, be disqualified from ever doing so."

— GORE VIDAL, AMERICAN WRITER

VOTER PUTDOWNS OF POLITICIANS

Perhaps one of the best putdowns of a politician came at the beginning of the last century when Republican presidential candidate Theodore Roosevelt was addressing a rally and found himself repeatedly interrupted by a drunk in the audience. The drunk kept shouting:

 "I'm a Democrat!"

Exasperated by the disruption to his speech, Roosevelt made the cardinal error of engaging with an intoxicated voter and asked:

 Why?

The drunk replied:

 "Because my grandfather was a Democrat and my father was a Democrat."

Roosevelt seeing the opening for a cutting putdown patiently nodded and said:

 "Let me ask you, Sir. If your grandfather had been a jackass and your father had been a jackass, what would you be?"

The drunk shot back.

 "A Republican!"

Other examples tend to be in the hit-and-run style of one-liners.

 "You've switched parties more times than a square dancer's partner!"

 "When it comes to foreign policy, weren't you just seen using a globe for the first time?"

 "Flexible on issues? You're more flexible than a Cirque du Soleil performer."

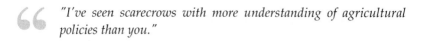

> *"I've seen scarecrows with more understanding of agricultural policies than you."*

> *"You couldn't run a bath, never mind a country."*

> *"It isn't your election to lose, it's ours to endure."*

> *"You would argue with a signpost and then head in the wrong direction."*

> *"A baby learns to talk in two years, but in later life some never learn when to be quiet."*

And the final word in this chapter goes to Henry Cate VII:

> *"The problem with political jokes is they get elected."*

* * *

Exploring the Art of Tongue-Fu

The art of putdowns, often associated with clever and biting wit, lies in the ability to deliver a cutting remark that simultaneously entertains and strikes a nerve. This is a delicate operation, walking a tightrope between adulation and alienation. Masters of this art form possess a keen sense of timing, wordplay, and situational awareness to create impactful and memorable insults. While it's important to approach this topic with caution, as putdowns can easily cross the line into cruelty, understanding the creative skill behind them can shed light on the dynamics of humour and social interaction.

When was this style of wordplay created and from whence did it come? This one is straightforward to answer and understand. When our disobedient progenitors succumbed in the Garden of Eden and ate fruit from the tree of good and evil, Paradise was lost and mankind would labour and use the knowledge, understanding and wisdom they had expropriated. Throughout the Scriptures, sage commentary and sharp observations, some dripping with searing contempt, is liberally scattered. Such criticisms tend to fall upon those who do evil or encourage and embolden others to do so.

 "O generation of vipers, who hath warned you to flee from the wrath to come?"

— John the Baptist

> *"Woe unto you, scribes and Pharisees, hypocrites! for ye compass sea and land to make one proselyte, and when he is made, ye make him twofold more the child of hell than yourselves."* [Matthew 23 v 15]

> *"Woe unto you, scribes and Pharisees, hypocrites! for ye are like unto whited sepulchres, which indeed appear beautiful outward, but are within full of dead men's bones, and of all uncleanness."* [Matthew 23 v 27]

> *"Ye serpents, ye generation of vipers, how can ye escape the damnation of hell?"* [Matthew 23 v 33]

For me, one of the cleverest and greatest putdowns in the Bible can be discovered when Jesus went unto the Mount of Olives. Scribes and Pharisees brought a woman "taken in adultery" and goaded him to accuse her, so she could be stoned as the law commanded.

> 6. *"But Jesus stooped down, and with his finger wrote on the ground, as though he heard them not.*
>
> 7. *So when they continued asking him, he lifted up himself, and said unto them, 'He that is without sin among you, let him first cast a stone at her.'*
>
> 8. *And again he stooped down, and wrote on the ground.*
>
> 9. *And they which heard it, being convicted by their own conscience, went out one by one, beginning at the eldest, even unto the last: and Jesus was left alone, and the woman standing in the midst.*
>
> 11. *And Jesus said unto her, 'Neither do I condemn thee: go, and sin no more.'"*
>
> — JOHN: CHAPTER 8

Various empires and cultures have come and gone, and all have contributed to the putdown art.

> *"Tell him, 'He who straps on his weapons had better not boast like one who takes them off.'"*

Some paid a heavy price. Cicero, like Demosthenes, often hurled insults in courts of law and in even more hallowed places. He not only insulted Mark Antony, but also turned his skill on the soon-to-be Augustus. Cicero stated that Octavius, as he was then known– "should be praised, honoured and disposed of".

Cicero was killed and his hands and head - those parts of his person that had inflicted the insults - were nailed up in public.

Let that be a warning to us all.

Putdowns, when executed skilfully, can elicit laughter and amusement. People enjoy clever wordplay and verbal sparring, and a well-crafted putdown can be seen as a display of intellectual prowess. Comedians, satirists, and quick-witted individuals often use putdowns to entertain and engage their audiences.

Knowing when and where to deliver a putdown is pivotal to maximising its impact. The element of surprise adds an extra layer of effectiveness, catching the recipient off-guard and amplifying the response.

If a political blowhard is seeking praise for his consistency, quoting Oscar Wilde might suffice:

 "Consistency is the last refuge of the unimaginative."

The art of putdowns often involves clever wordplay, puns, and double entendres. Crafting a remark that is both humorous and demeaning requires linguistic skill and creativity. A carefully chosen turn of phrase can enhance the impact of the insult and make it more memorable.

Some putdowns serve as a form of social commentary, highlighting absurdities, hypocrisy, or contradictions. By using humour and irony, individuals can draw attention to flaws, shortcomings, or negative behaviours in others or certain aspects of society. However, it is essential to differentiate between constructive criticism and mean-spirited insults.

While putdowns can be an art form, ethical concerns also come into play. It is crucial to consider the effect of our words on others and be mindful of the potential harm caused by the wisecrack. Crossing the line from playful banter into malice and bullying can have long-lasting negative consequences on relationships and individuals' mental well-being. I cannot think that the artist, John Constable, was attempting to find a safe passage through that gap when he commented:

 "The world is rid of Lord Byron, but the deadly slime of his touch still remains."

Ouch!

The effectiveness and acceptability of slights depend on the context and audience. What may be humorous banter among friends might be deeply hurtful in a different setting. Taking into consideration the sensitivity and emotional state of the recipient is vital to gauge the appropriateness of a putdown. I suspect we're often so outraged by an event that our anger is not just the prime but the only focus of our expression. This was the probable scenario when the Prince of Wales (now King Charles III) declared the extension to the National Gallery to be:

 "A monstrous carbuncle on the face of a much-loved and elegant friend."

If my assessment of architectural magnificence was the barometer, the then Prince was 'spot on'. However, if I'd been the architect, I would have been severely crestfallen and demoralised and might have avoided going into work for a few days.

Let us next consider the disarming charm of witty putdowns. In the thrilling realm of verbal jousting, where the sharpest wit reigns supreme, the art of the putdown could be likened to a sophisticated, if somewhat merciless, form of linguistic ballet. Balancing between wit and rudeness, it's that Penelope Pitstop-meets-Walter Matthau spectacle, an electrifying elixir of smarts and sass. Rest assured, when handled by an adroit daredevil of words, it can create an exhilarating and lasting result.

Picture a pie of humour, served piping hot with a side of snark – that's the art of putdowns for you. Possessing an allure that extends beyond the stale realm of mere insults, skilled putdownologists (my contribution for inclusion in the next Webster's dictionary) utilise a Swiss Army Knife of tactics. They can practise laugh-inducing humour, impeccable timing, cunning wordplay, and ruthless honesty, to construct their pinpoint-accurate jabs.

Envisage the putdown as a party trick. It whips up a cocktail of laughter and amusement, brilliantly showcasing intellectual acrobatics. The audience guffaws not only at the victim's expense, but also at the wit and cunning concealed within the sharp quip. Who needs a stand-up routine when a single smartly crafted putdown can knock 'em dead?

Witty putdowns aren't just about diminishing egos, they're also a dazzling display of word-smithery, heart-racing rhymes, droll puns, and curious connotations that weave the tapestry of a scathing but delightful syllabic burn. This is where Shakespeare and Eminem can share the same stage.

Some putdowns turn into incisive satirical commentary, slicing through societal absurdities more easily than a Ginsu knife through a can. By highlighting the missteps and follies of others, a well-placed jibe paves the way for laughter, reflection, and maybe even reform. Take a TV Presenter's quip about Tory MP Jeffrey Archer:

 "Jeffrey Archer has issued a strenuous denial – that's as good as a signed confession really."

Surprisingly, putdowns can also be used for bonding and creating togetherness in certain social groups. When used playfully among friends who understand and appreciate the dynamic, putdowns can serve as a form of light-hearted banter, promoting a sense of shared humour and camaraderie.

Don't draw back in horror just yet, though! Not all putdowns are stealthy uppercuts. Many a jest, discharged within friendly circles, sets the stage for camaraderie and shared chuckles. This supports the strange, paradoxical idea that a friendly dig can also serve as a bonding adhesive – nontoxic verbal super-glue. We refer to this variety as "teasing" or "banter" and it often signals familiarity and friendship.

Balancing on the razor's edge between witty banter and outright bullying can be perilous, and we shall look at this issue in a later chapter. When this teasing mockery comes across as calculated but convivial, in my country, it's called "having a bit of craic". This admittedly gets unusual reactions from visitors who have a different perspective on how an evening of "having a bit of craic" might end.

In my homeland, we have very high tolerance levels for how extreme this "friendly banter" can get. We have perfected the art, and outsiders often hold their breath when comments that appear to them to be ill-placed rudeness and personal slurs are fired. Before long, they soon relax and, like expectant tennis spectators, eagerly anticipate the revenge backhand smash. Before they leave our shores, most will have embraced and incorporated the art style into their conversations, which must make for a fun transition when they return to their homes.

Not everyone's pallet has been reconfigured and developed to appreciate such seasoned game meat, however. For many, a poorly judged comment can tip the scales towards damage and distress, turning laughter into hurt. Hence, in this gung-ho world of putdowns, it becomes vital to remember that, while quick comebacks might earn you a badge, a broken friendship could feel more like a self-inflicted wound.

Putdowns are chameleons, their impact swinging dramatically with context and audience. A jab can be a playful buddy-nudge at a pub but transform into a clout on the jaw in a different setting. Just as the joker among friends may not be the maestro at a funeral, context is key.

If there is ever an environment within which maximum care is required when attempting to deliver an interview terminating impact, it is during a serious conflict with global ramifications. Yet a spokesman for the Israeli army stepped into that minefield during the war against Hamas in Gaza:

"Would you forgive these terrorists?"

— CNN Iɴᴛᴇʀᴠɪᴇᴡᴇʀ

"No, my job isn't to forgive. Forgiveness belongs to God. God will decide whether to forgive them. My job is to arrange their meeting."

— IDF Gᴇɴᴇʀᴀʟ

I am inclined to think that reader opinions of the General's remark will, at least to some extent, depend on their view of the war itself and its conduct. Some will believe it was a fitting response to an inappropriate question, considering Hamas had invaded Israel murdering women, children, and elderly non-combatants. Others will harbour resentment that while the IDF was pounding the Gaza Strip with artillery someone exhibited a lack of apprehension while speaking about extinguishing peoples' lives. It might be said that this was a soldier and not a politician answering. However, in this instance the General knew which constituency he was addressing and how it would be received by his target audience, and equally, he would have been aware of the disquiet his confidence would have on his enemies.

To tie it all together, a well-conjured putdown is a high-wire act of communication entertainment, wordplay, and social navigation. Hence, the most vital apparatus in our toolkit is the aptitude to know and understand what both a witty comment and a withering slight look like, and the difference between the two.

* * *

Putdowns as Entertainment

Comedy – Stand-up or Sit-Com

The humorous yet knifing remarks often relayed with practised deftness by comedians, have long been a fundamental aspect of comedic tradition. They serve as mechanisms to enhance a jovial atmosphere, broaden audience connections, or even assert dominance over a discourse when necessary. In the broader sense of the comedy landscape, these insults aren't specifically intended to wound, but instead to tap into shared human experiences or absurdities, creating unified laughter that transcends differences. From the sly observational wisecracks of comedians like Groucho Marx, to the scathing social commentaries of comedians like George Carlin, the use of humorously offensive language, strategically employed, has formed the backbone of much modern comedic narrative.

In the context of sitcom humour, these insults often function as catchphrases or running gags, distinguishing figures, and contributing to their unique identities. Sitcoms thrive on the dynamism of interpersonal relationships, and comedy insults play a pivotal role here. Characters like Sheldon Cooper in "The Big Bang Theory" or Chandler Bing in "Friends", for instance, owe much of their charm to the crafty and witty insults they deploy, shaping the laugh track of each series. In these scenarios, the insults are aimed at other characters within the sitcom universe and are typically scripted to avoid sparking genuine hostility between actors.

Stand-up comedy, on the other hand, presents a different approach. Stand-up comedians, mostly working with live audiences, have a freer rein to target their insults. The classic trope of "heckler takedowns" represents a perfect use of real-time insults against disruptive audience members. Alternatively, comedians sometimes playfully target those who arrive late to their shows – a gentle (or at times not so gentle) reproof, establishing control while keeping the tone light. If you doubt me, just reserve a front row seat for a stand-up comedian's performance and try arriving late. Then watch as the act pauses, and you and your companion are addressed from the stage:

> *"Did you two have a fight in the parking lot?"*

> *"Were you waiting for your wife to go to sleep before you picked this one up?"*

> *"Were you getting your hair done, dear? Try another salon next time."*

> *"Ohhh! You poor girl. I take it you're on a blind date?"*

Or, from the regular stock of the great Belfast comic James Young:

> *"Your hair's beautiful, love. Who knitted it?"*

If the late arrival includes someone wearing particularly gaudy or outlandish clothes:

> *"I love your outfit, missus."* (Inevitably, the audience starts chuckling.) *"Stop it! Stop it! That's not nice. We've all been at rummage sales."*

While a stand-up comedian's putdown of latecomers is often in the form of a question, the unfortunate souls have no prospect of delivering a riposte that will be heard. They can only display their finest simulated smile and sit down before their slow pace becomes a target for another putdown.

A strategically placed insult in stand-up can land a big blast, establish persona, or create an interactive dynamic unique to the immediacy and unpredictability of live performance. Importantly, the beauty of these insults in stand-up lies in their purpose – to make people laugh and create an inclusive atmosphere, where the insult is part of the shared joke, rather than a personal attack.

Comedians rely on their wits to elicit laughter and engage audiences. A well-crafted joke or a clever one-liner can determine the success or failure of a performance. By skilfully observing the world around them and finding humour in everyday situations, comedians can shed light on deeper truths and make audiences see things from a different perspective. Often, the performer will use humorous putdowns pointed towards traits that many in the audience will share. Still, everyone can join in the laughter as no lights are flashing above the heads of those who are being ridiculed.

Interestingly, when we tune in to pop culture, insults have become the backbone of comedy – the famed "roasts", the snarky sitcom characters, the sarcastic heroes. They're supposed to be hilarious, showcase wit, and entertain, but the projection of these exchanges in real-life gets as complicated as untangling Christmas tree lights.

Pop culture wisecracks are a common way for movies, TV shows, and music to inject humour and create memorable moments. These examples display creative analogies, exaggerated comparisons, and playful language to deliver the insults in an entertaining manner. By using pop culture references, these putdowns not only amuse audiences, but also demonstrate a deep knowledge and understanding of the current cultural landscape. In TV shows and movies, the narratives of witty, sarcastic characters who readily throw taunts are often celebrated.

Insults have always been a part of human interaction, and pop culture, with its vast influence, has provided us with a treasure trove of memorable putdowns. Whether it's the quick wit of characters in movies, sarcastic remarks on TV shows, or biting lyrics in music, insults have become an art form in themselves.

Movies and Misdemeanours

Films have played a significant role in shaping pop culture putdowns. Some insults have become iconic, leaving an indelible mark on audiences. Films like "Mean Girls" and "Clueless" have given birth to memorable phrases that have since permeated everyday language. Quotes like "That's so fetch!" and "As if!" serve as quick comebacks, allowing viewers to participate in the verbal sparring that occurs onscreen.

Insults in movies often come in the form of clever one-liners, showcasing the wit and sharpness of the characters. Scripts are carefully crafted to include jibes that embody the traits of a character or their relationship dynamics. From the razor-sharp barbs used in "The Devil Wears Prada" to the banter-filled dialogue of "The Social Network," insults in movies not only entertain, but also reveal the complexities of the characters from which they originate.

"I envy people who have never met you."

— THE PROPOSAL

"You have a face for radio and a voice for silent movies."

— MONSTERS, INC.

"You may not be the dumbest person in the world, but you'd better hope they don't die."

— GHOSTBUSTERS

"I can't even find a suitable insult for you, you unfathomable twit."

— THE IMPORTANCE OF BEING EARNEST

"If I threw a stick, you'd leave, right?"

— THOR

"I have a lot of respect for people who do things I could never do . . . like talking to you."

— THE HANGOVER

> *"If they took the IQ of all the people in this room, and added them together, it still wouldn't reach room temperature."*

— Beetlejuice

> *"In one scene I have to hit her in the face, and I thought we could save some money on sound effects here."*

— Ken Wall on Bette Midler, both acting in Jinxed

In addition to the carefully scripted putdowns and studied insults many other movie-related celebrities appear in the zinger list of credits.

> *"There was no one remotely like John Houston (film director), except, maybe, Lucifer."*

— Doris Lilly, Writer, and Newspaper Columnist

> *"Kirk would be the first to tell you that he's a difficult man; I would be the second."*

— Burt Lancaster on Kirk Douglas

> *"His ears made him look like a taxicab with both doors open."*

— Howard Hughes on Actor Clarke Gable

> Earl Wilson, politician: *"Have you ever been mistaken for a man?"*
>
> Tallulah Bankhead: *"No darling, have you?"*

> Party Guest: *"I haven't seen you for 41 years."*
>
> Tallulah Bankhead: *"I thought I told you to wait in the car."*

> *"Richard Gere and Cindy Crawford – he's elastic and she's plastic."*

— Sandra Berthed, Comedian

"Elizabeth Taylor has more chins than the Chinese telephone directory."

— JOAN RIVERS, COMEDIAN

"He loves nature in spite of what it did to him."

— FORREST TUCKER

"Peter Sellers was his own worst enemy, although there was plenty of competition."

— ROY BOULTING, FILM DIRECTOR

"Would you ever consider keeping your clothes on if the script demanded it?"

— PAUL KAY, TO DEMI MOORE

"Which part is he playing now?"

— SOMERSET MAUGHAM, ON SPENCER TRACY DURING THE FILMING OF DR JEKYLL AND MR HYDE

"He can light up a room just by leaving it."

— BOB HOPE

"He has the attention span of a lightning bolt."

— ROBERT REDFORD

"Hollywood: a place where they shoot too many pictures and not enough actors."

— WALTER WINCHELL, COMMENTATOR

TV TAKEDOWNS

TV shows have their fair share of memorable insults, with some catchphrases becoming cultural touchstones. Iconic characters like Tyrion Lannister from "Game of Thrones" are known for their sharp tongues and biting remarks. These characters have become fan favourites because of their unique ability to deliver hilarious, sarcastic, and sometimes thought-provoking insults. My choice of Lannister quip is:

 "It's hard to put a leash on a dog once you've put a crown on its head."

Insults during TV shows often serve as comic relief or contribute to character development. In other shows, insults are their *raison d'etre*. Wisecracks can shape the dynamics between characters and create memorable moments that fans eagerly discuss. Shows like "The Weakest Link", "The Thick of It", "Blackadder", "Father Ted", "Derry Girls", "Fawlty Towers" and "Only Fools and Horses" thrive on insult-laden exchanges between characters, pushing the boundaries, while eliciting laughter from their audiences. Come to think of it, these are my favourite shows. What does that say about me?

TV is also the target of insults. The number claiming ownership of the following quote testifies to it being a popular viewpoint. I choose to credit it to an American comedian and actor.

 "TV is called a 'medium' because so little of it is either rare or well done!"

— ERNIE KOVACS

 "What do ITV and fish fingers have in common? After two or three minutes, you have to turn them over."

— FRANK SKINNER

 "Television has proved that people will look at anything rather than each other."

— ANN LANDERS

"I must say I find television very educational. The minute somebody turns it on, I go into the library and read a good book."

— GROUCHO MARX

"Television is 'real'. It is immediate, it has dimension. It tells you what to think and blasts it in. It must be right. It seems so right. It rushes you on so quickly to its own conclusions, your mind hasn't time to protest, what nonsense!"

— RAY BRADBURY

"All television is educational. The question is: what is it teaching?"

— NICHOLAS JOHNSON

TV show hosts, presenters, and participants all happily compete for the insult crown:

"As you know, Tom Cruise and Katie Holmes had a baby girl. It weighs seven pounds and is twenty inches long ... wait, that's Tom."

— DAVID LETTERMAN, TV TALK-SHOW HOST

"Like Anne Robinson (TV Host) in a Korean restaurant. It's dog eat dog."

— GRAHAM NORTON, COMEDIAN

"You're so basic, you make vanilla seem wild."

— TV SHOW: PARKS AND RECREATION

"You're not pretty enough to be this stupid."

— OLIVIA WILDE, HOUSE

"I would love to insult you, but I'm afraid I won't do as well as nature did."

      — Steve Martin, Roxanne

"It has been reported that Spain is the number one consumer of cocaine in the world. Apparently, Spain narrowly beat Kate Moss."

      — Conan O'Brien, Talk-Show Host

"She's so boring. Her natural state is flatlining."

      — Ruby Wax on Jennifer Saunders

"I'm sorry, but I can't take you seriously with that haircut."

"Did you fall from heaven? Because it looks like you landed on your face."

"Somewhere out there, there's a tree working tirelessly to provide oxygen for you. Go apologise."

"I see your sense of humour bypass surgery was a success."

"It's not you, it's your personality. Actually, no, it's definitely you."

"I don't need Google, I have you to answer all my dumb questions."

"It's impressive how you consistently find new ways to lower the bar."

"I don't mind talking to you; it's listening to you, that's the problem."

"Your presence is about as welcome as a porcupine in a balloon factory."

And here's evidence that sometimes radio and television stars don't put a stop to their mocking, even at the end of the victim's life.

 "It proves what they always say: give the public what they want to see, and they'll come out for it."

> — RED SKELTON ON THE CROWDS AT THE FUNERAL OF HARRY COHN (COFOUNDER COLUMBIA PICTURES).

MUSIC WITHOUT HARMONY

Music, too, is a platform for artists to express their emotions, including anger and frustration, through lyrics that can be interpreted as insults. From diss tracks in hip-hop to breakup songs in various genres, insults in music have the power to cut deep and resonate with audiences.

In the world of hip-hop, artists engage in battles through rap, where insults are skilfully woven into verses to assert dominance over opponents. Examples of such legendary battles include Tupac vs. Notorious B.I.G. and Eminem vs. Machine Gun Kelly. These confrontations have given birth to some of the most scathing insults in music history.

Pop music includes less antagonistic but still caustic lines as the following pop song lyrics show.

"Your singing voice could dry out a lake."

"Your jokes are as flat as day-old soda."

"Your dance moves are so stiff, you make Frankenstein look like Baryshnikov."

"Your fashion choices are a crime against humanity."

These genres also use insults to convey personal experiences or social commentary. Artists like Taylor Swift and Alanis Morissette are known for their poignant breakup songs, where they cleverly insult former lovers, while expressing their own pain and growth. These songs provide catharsis for listeners who share feelings of heartache and resentment. Alongside putdown lyrics there are other discordant tones from those associated with music in its many forms.

> *"I don't like country music, but I don't mean to denigrate those who do; and for the people who like country music, denigrate means 'put down'."*

— Bob Newhart, Comedian

> *"I liked your opera. I think I will set it to music."*

— Beethoven to a Fellow Composer

Stage and Scream

From stage actors, producers, writers and critics, the use of putdowns is no less acid than in any other aspect of entertainment.

> Dustin Farnum: *"I've never been better! In the last act yesterday, I had the audience glued to their seats."*
>
> Oliver Herford: *"How clever of you to think of it."*

> *"The Silent Witness is not a bad play, though hardly a good play. . . Miss Strozzi had the temerity to wear as truly horrible a gown as I have ever seen on the American stage. Had she not luckily been strangled by a member of the cast while disporting this garment, I should have fought my way to the stage and done her in, myself."*

— Dorothy Parker on actor Kay Strozzi

> *"When Mr Wilbur calls his play 'Halfway to Hell' he underestimates the distance."*

— Brooks Atkinson, Critics

> Diner displaying food on the end of his fork: *"Is this pig?"*
>
> Douglas Jerrold, playwright: *"To which end of the fork do you refer?"*

> *"I clapped because it's finished, not because I like it."*

— Critic

> "He writes his plays for the ages – the ages between five and twelve."

— GEORGE JEAN NATHAN ON GEORGE BERNARD SHAW

> "For those who missed it the first time, this is your golden opportunity: you can miss it again."

— MICHAEL BILLINGTON, CRITIC, ON THE MUSICAL GODSPELL

POP CULTURE

Pop culture putdowns have had a profound impact on both show business and society. Memorable insults have become part of our everyday lexicon, imitated in conversations, and shared on social media platforms. They create moments that fans relish, fostering a sense of community and shared experience.

Furthermore, they can reflect and shape societal attitudes. They offer commentary on gender, race, class, and other social constructs, highlighting the power dynamics and prejudices that exist within our society. By examining these insults, we can gain insights into the underlying social issues and engage in meaningful conversations about them.

However, the line between playful banter and harmful insults can be blurred. It is essential to distinguish between the fictional world of entertainment and real-life interactions. Insults that work in a fictional context may not necessarily translate well to real-world situations. Responsible consumption of pop culture puts us in a position to appreciate the creativity and entertainment value, while recognising the need for respect and empathy in our personal relationships.

* * *

THE PSYCHOLOGY OF PUTDOWNS

As we traverse the multifaceted terrain of earthly discourse, it becomes crucial to understand the role of negative language forms, such as insults and putdowns. These negative strategies are prevalent in both interpersonal and group communication, reflecting aggression, competition and, sometimes, humour. The text surrounding these interactions may often be an exercise in degradation but, it might be argued, it provides a key to understanding fundamental strands of human nature.

Our starting point is to explore why individuals resort to insults and putdowns, decoding the complex psychological and social nuances involved. Yet, we must also stop to consider the impact of causing linguistic lacerations on the defenceless.

To explore this sphere, we delve into two major realms: psychology and social dynamics.

The truth is that we humans, like actors in a never-ending daytime soap opera, have a peculiar fondness for insults and putdowns – when they are guided towards others. They're peppered throughout our daily dialogues, like a dash of chilli to spice up idle talk. But why are we so drawn to these verbal jabs? Buckle up, as we embark on this tumultuous tour of tacky tongue-lashing.

First up, we trespass into the territory of psychology. Here, we uncover the startling reality that we humans throw insults because our egos won't quit. We often disguise our insecurities behind a barrage of bluster, using insults as our shields and putdowns as our swords. It's the ego's personal talent show, auditioning for validation and dominance. Heard of the saying, "A good offence is the best defence"? Well, forget the football field – this is the critical strategy in the insult-hurler's playbook. People who can't afford a Bugatti, yacht, and private island can assert their dominance in a budget-friendly way: by using insults and putdowns. It's a fairly handy survival trick from our cave-dwelling days, akin to puffing out your chest to seem more substantial to that sabre-tooth tiger eyeing you for lunch.

Additionally, psychologists have noted the role of "displacement" in this context. Displacement is the phenomenon where an individual directs negative emotions or aggression towards others, rather than dealing with the true source of their discomfort. Like a magician misdirecting the audience, displacement allows the agitated soul to transfer their drama onto the target, instead of dealing with the anxiety that is really pulling the strings. There is a simple logic to this behaviour. "Why punch a wall and hurt myself, when I can mentally punch others with words and hurt them instead?" Misery loves company, they say, and boy, those headshrinkers aren't always wrong.

Dare we delve into the square dance of social dynamics? Here, we find the Insult Olympics, a social structure, with its jungle law and hunger games, in which contenders vie for position and resources, often resembling a manic market of malevolence. It's not uncommon to see Bob subtly denigrating Fred's stellar work just, to increase his chances of securing the promotion.

Society, with its layered power dynamics and incessant struggle for a bigger share of the pie, unknowingly incubates a fertile ground for insults to proliferate. Samuel Johnson didn't hold back by conforming to the niceties of fair play:

 "Treating your adversary with respect is giving him an advantage to which he is not entitled."

It won't take much pulling at the threads of our societal fabric to recognise that it often encourages competition and comparison, whether in schools, workplaces, or even within families. This imbues individuals with the motivation to diminish others to uplift themselves, which can easily manifest in the form of putdowns.

Furthermore, people sometimes offend their colleagues in a sometimes-misguided attempt at bonding or nurturing camaraderie, in the belief that shared ridicule unifies a group. It seems about as effective as knitting with noodles, doesn't it? Yet some can participate in the cut and thrust quite merrily. Consider Oscar Wilde and James McNeill Whistler. On hearing Whistler make a witty remark:

> Wilde: *"I wish I'd said that!"*
>
> Whistler: *"You will, Oscar, you will!"*

Then on another occasion:

> Whistler: *"I went past your house this afternoon."*
>
> Wilde: *"Thank you."*

Because they were friends, and both enjoyed exercising their wit and injecting amusing satire, no offence was ever taken – or at least ever acknowledged.

For the less combative, derogatory remarks may have a powerful psychological impact on both the person delivering and the one receiving them. These negative remarks can be overt or subtle, but their purpose is often to belittle, demean, or diminish the self-esteem of the recipient. Understanding the psychology behind putdowns sheds light on why some engage in this behaviour and the effects it can have.

While the deliverers of putdowns and insults may gain some temporary satisfaction at having relieved their frustration, their actions, when targeted at those not accustomed to plying that trade, can occasion significant psychological and emotional effects. How often, when we have been on the wrong end of the putdown gun barrel, have we questioned the reliability of the rhyme our mothers taught us?

> *Sticks and stones might break my bones*
>
> *But words shall never hurt me.*

We all know, no matter whether we are sensitive flowers or we have rhino skin, that it can hurt – particularly if there is a grain of truth contained in the insult. It can lead to decreased self-esteem, feelings of inadequacy, anxiety, depression, and, if repeated persistently in severe cases, even contribute to the development of mental health issues. Frequent exposure to putdowns can erode an individual's sense of worth and make them question their abilities and value as a person.

In dissecting the reasons for insult and putdown use, we reach a point where we can identify and delight in timely, clever, and humorous putdowns in a context where the victim and the environment mesh. We can distinguish them from vulgar, scorched earth, hurtful abuse, aimed at unarmed and undeserving civilians. This vital understanding paves the way for a better appreciation of how and when it is beneficial and appropriate to unsheathe the stiletto.

If I were to say to a seasoned politician:

 "Being with you is like being in a room with a vampire and not having a crucifix,"

he or she might be conspicuously pleased. It suggests they're an alpha personality, feared by their opponents and capable of tearing their foes apart. If, on the other hand, I was to say it to my dear Aunt Mabel she would be horrified, sorely pained, and probably cry for weeks.

Against this background, it seems acceptable and demonstrably unavoidable that the main practitioners of the art will come from the worlds of politics, the law and entertainment. In these arenas, verbal jabs reign supreme and snarky comebacks are the currency of conversations, debates, and performances. On these stages, the absence of barbed putdowns is as rare as a dodo sighting and as infrequent as a three-toed sloth's potty breaks. Few who choose these careers will open the door and enter without the expectation of engaging in wit and word warfare. On the insult battlefield, these warriors compete to be the most prolific and pre-eminent in the Petri dish of putdowns. Personally, my money is on the politicians.

Two of these disciplines clashed when Bernard Shaw wrote to Winston Churchill:

Shaw: *"I am enclosing two tickets to the first night of my new play; bring a friend . . . if you have one."*

Churchill: *"Cannot possibly attend first night; will attend second, if there is one."*

But why limit yourself to putting down an individual, when you could take out a whole cadre of people?

"America will always do the right thing, but only after it has exhausted all the alternatives."

— Winston Churchill, PM

"The problem with socialism is that you eventually run out of other people's money."

— Margaret Thatcher, PM

The same can be said of the multitude of nationalistic and racial insults where the insulter magnifies a supposed defect or peculiarity in a national characteristic.

"Much may be made of a Scotchman, if he be caught young."

— Samuel Johnston

"The Irish are a fair people; they never speak well of one another."

— Samuel Johnston

"If one could only teach the English how to talk and the Irish how to listen, society would be quite civilised."

— Oscar Wilde

"I am willing to love all mankind, except an American."

— Samuel Johnston

"I have seen their backs before."

— THE DUKE OF WELLINGTON ON THE FRENCH WHO, STILL
SMARTING FROM THEIR DEFEAT, TURNED THEIR BACKS ON HIM

 "I may be Irish, but I'm not stupid."

— PRESIDENT JOE BIDEN

Among the most insulted professions are politicians, lawyers, estate agents/realtors and used-car salespeople. I can attest to this: I started my adult life selling houses, then while working on a law degree, I was elected to Parliament – anyone want to buy my car?

FREEDOM FROM THE PRESS

So, let's leave those professions alone, for now, and turn to (or on) journalism – if, journalism does indeed merit that classification. It will provide us with ripe pickings. Mark Twain is credited with saying:

 "If you don't read the newspaper you are uninformed, if you do read the newspaper you are misinformed."

 "The four pillars of wisdom that support journalistic endeavours are lies, stupidity, money-grubbing and ethical irresponsibility."

— MARLON BRANDO, ACTOR

 "Newspaper editors are men who separate the wheat from the chaff, and then print the chaff."

— ADLAI STEVENSON

There's always someone who was out of class when the discussion took place about showing respect for the dead. General William Sherman is said to have reacted to a report of the death of three reporters by shellfire:

 "Good! Now we shall have news from hell before breakfast."

Time has changed nothing; journalists are still an easy, warranted, and legitimate target. Stephen Fry thought so, anyway:

 "Many people would no more think of entering journalism than the sewage business – which at least does some good."

* * *

Putdowns and
the Law

The legal profession has been the butt of many enjoyable jokes. It's fascinating that, on this balance sheet, there are few lawyers coming to defend their cause. No doubt there are more victims of the law than lawyers (although some would argue there are plenty of them to go around). Yet it does leave one wondering why it is so. Is it because lawyers think, by keeping their heads down, we will not notice them and therefore vent our spleen on some other profession? Alternatively, have they calculated that, if they aren't getting paid for their wit, why expend energy on such unprofitable matters?

Lawyers might suggest that they are above such base behaviour, or they would not wish to stoop to mixing with the masses. We are forced to accept that the arena within which they perform is deliberately stern and serious and it is hard to have the courtroom falling about in laughter as a 10-year sentence is being imposed. My experience of lawyers is that they aren't a humourless bunch ... group. (What is the collective term for lawyers? — No! Let's not go down that road).

Except, perhaps, to allow Woodrow Wilson to interject:

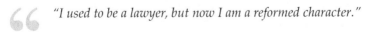 *"I used to be a lawyer, but now I am a reformed character."*

Yet, in less serious times and for less serious crimes, the humour and repartee do surface. A sage and vastly experienced "silk", being lectured by a "wet behind the ears" young lawyer, calmly dismissed the pretender:

66   *"I am not young enough to know everything."*

Alternatively, there is the honest assertion that reads like an insult:

66   *"Law school taught me one thing; how to take two situations that are exactly the same and show how they are different."*

                        — HART POMERANTZ, CANADIAN LAWYER.

And then there is the honest assertion that receives a response intended as an insult:

66   Judge: *"I am sorry, Mr Smith, but I am none the wiser."*

         Smith: *"No, my Lord. But you are better informed."*

              — F. E. SMITH AFTER SUMMARISING HIS CASE TO A CONFUSED
                                               JUDGE.

JUDICIAL AND LAWYERLY PUTDOWNS

I'm taking no risks with these quotes, given the field in which I am grazing, so I shall avoid attributing any of the "exhibits".

66   *"Your Honour, I'd like to present Exhibit 'A': my client's alibi. Or as the prosecution might call it, 'inconvenient evidence'."*

66   *"Objection, your Honour – counsel is leading the witness, the jury, and a parade down Main Street with his line of questioning."*

66   *"It appears my colleague is hurling accusations faster than a short-order cook tosses pancakes."*

66   *"If rumour were evidence, Your Honour, we'd also have to debate my client's apparent habit of turning water into wine."*

66   *"Your Honour, if we took a break every time my colleague distorted the truth, court hours would be over before they*

started."

Judge: "Where's your client?"

Lawyer: "Presumably feeling grateful that he's far away from this line of questioning, Your Honour."

"If we could gain a dollar for every time counsel's argument made leaps of logic, we'd have funded the judiciary budget by now."

Lawyer: "My client is as guilty of these charges as I am of understatement."

"I'd like to remind my esteemed colleague that trial by combat was outlawed in the 19th century."

"I'd say this case is as open-and-shut as my opponent's mind appears to be."

"Your Honour, are you familiar with the term 'jury of your peers'? My client feels he'd have a fairer trial being judged by a collection of the neighbourhood's stray cats."

"Your Honour, if interruptions were evidence, the prosecution would've won the case by now."

"And here I thought counsel brought their mountain of paperwork to present a case, not hide behind it."

"If my opponent's argument were a book, it'd surely be shelved under fiction."

"Next time, I'll remember to bring a ladder, perhaps then I'd be able to reach my opponent's conclusions."

"Counsel's keeping his cards so close to his chest, it's a wonder he can breathe, Your Honour."

"If I wanted a crash course on diversionary tactics, I would've taken a magic class with Houdini, not counsel."

66 *"If you squint hard enough, and tilt your head just right, you might be able to see my opponent's point."*

66 *"Your Honour, will there be a height limit imposed on the prosecutor's leaps of logic?"*

66 *"I've seen better cases on antique roadshows."*

66 *"When real evidence is ready to make an appearance, do let me know."*

66 *"You're as familiar with the truth as a cat is with algebra."*

Putdowns From Witnesses Who Don't Fear a Prison Term

66 *"You say you're the judge, but my mother always told me I'd be judged by higher powers."*

66 *"Sorry, I forgot my crystal ball today; I can't be of help with future events, counsel."*

66 *"Do I come to your workplace and ask you ridiculous questions?"*

66 *"I may be on the stand, but it's quite clear we're all on trial here."*

66 *"Roe v. Wade? I thought that was a debate about rivers."*

66 *"Last time someone dug a hole this deep, they found dinosaur fossils."*

66 *"Am I the only one waiting for the punchline here, or is it just bad comedy?"*

66 *"I see now why Lady Justice is blindfolded; it's to avoid your sartorial choices."*

66 *"You have twisted this story more than a pretzel baker, counsel."*

* * *

Responding to
Putdowns – The
Alternatives

When confronted with the prospect of jousting with jokers or duelling with devils, it is wise, before choosing from a well-stocked store of options for dealing out a zinger, to undertake a prompt evaluation. The issues to be calculated should be as follows.

Is the duel in the "exempt professions" category?

I regard some professions as necessarily relying on wordcraft. We have dealt with three of them – politics, entertainment, and the law. If this is your stage, then it's not about whether, but how you respond. In this category, putdowns are not only common but expected. A failure to respond in most cases will be regarded as a victory to your opponent.

Is your opponent your equal?

There is little upside to brutally taking down an inferior opponent. A vicious reply might gain them sympathy. I don't say you shouldn't respond – that may be determined by the answer to the next calculation, but if you take up the cudgels, do so with wit and without malice. Don't let them win through pity.

Is the remark deliberate or unintentional?

If you conclude the comment, while hurtful, wasn't designed to cause harm, you may wish to let it lie and speak privately with the individual on some later occasion. If it is deemed to be a deliberate insult, then you may wish to escalate the matter to the next calculation.

Is the person sober or drunk, *compos mentis*, a fool, or trying to rattle you?

Never argue with a drunk or a lunatic; it is beneath you – not even for a laugh, unless they persist and there's someone to remove them from your space. If you respond, they are likely to continue the dialogue if they're still in place. Remember this adage:

 "Don't argue with fools, because people from a distance can't tell which one is you."

Be even more careful if you glean that the intention of the agitator is to provoke you – they may be wanting to unsettle you, and make you respond inappropriately by losing your cool or focus. Digs are often designed to score rather than amuse, to worm their way under your skin, intended more for decimation than for humour. Take care! The nature of this ambush style has the characteristics of a dark alley late at night, echoing with the chilling laughter of a hyena. It's a place where casual onlookers might need an emotional flak jacket to avoid the shrapnel, the witty remarks carrying ammunition designed to wound the pride. Be on your guard as you move to the next calculation.

Is it banter or an insult?

Here, some options are available. If it's banter, you can smile and offer a resigned shake of the head or return some light-hearted ribbing. In this context, a friendly, jovial exchange is as harmless as a pillow fight. Whereas, if it's good-natured joshing, hurling back a cutting riposte would be unwise and disruptive of your relationship with the teaser. If it is judged to be an insult, you can choose to ignore it, as if the view of the perpetrator is of no consequence. If you decide to respond, then how you do so will depend on a further calculation.

IS IT WITTY OR VENOMOUS?

We are, at this stage, still leaving open the option of a non-response, but you must be readying the rejoinder. The rule here is simple — a witty remark deserves a witty response — if you can think of one. A vicious attack can be de-escalated with either a witty response or no response. It can also be met blow for blow. How to determine the appropriate reaction depends on the next evaluation.

IS THE PERSON'S DEMEANOUR AGGRESSIVE OR FRIENDLY, LOUD, OR CALM?

This will determine the nature and tone of any interaction. While aggressive personalities are seldom appeased by amiable answers, whether you respond in kind may be determined by the next calculation.

IS THERE AN AUDIENCE YOU NEED TO CONSIDER?

It is much easier to walk away if there's no viewing public. Nothing but your pride is at stake in refusing to engage. A dismissive wave of the hand or a "get a life" quip is the most that is needed if this is the option you pick. With an audience, no matter how small, you have other determinations to make. How will your failure to retaliate impact upon people's judgement of your views and position? Also, will they accept the validity of the putdown if you don't counter it? Just as significant is the consideration: will people see you as an easy target for their insults if you don't take this person on?

IS THERE A HIDDEN MOTIVATION BEHIND THE INSULT?

If you know the individual or suspect they represent a particular viewpoint, the likelihood is that you are being set up or played. The jab may only be a means to an end. It may be the bait to goad you into a revealing or damaging reply. Your knowledge of where you are being led must alert and guide you in which direction to take.

READY OR NOT

This step-by-step guide may seem to require a huge delay in presenting your reply, but with practice, you will determine all these factors during the time the person is directing the putdown at you.

Remember, in making your choices, playful banter holds a magnifying mirror to human quirks and foibles, amplifying them through the lens of harmless jest. On the contrary, intentional insults, attired in the dark cloak of malice, aim to scour self-esteem, an unwelcome denizen crawling into the peace of social interactions.

You will have to choose between the Old Testament 'eye for an eye' doctrine or the New Testament exhortation to 'turn the other cheek'. So, make your decision whether to render no response, de-escalate, provide a light touch or humorous repost, or go onto a war footing. No response requires no comment. Comebacks that merit a feather duster approach can be mined from the many examples contained in these pages, until you have fine-tuned your own strategy and accompanying skill.

But before we go on to consider a range of other light-touch tactics or you decide to enter the no-holds-barred arena – a passing word about my experiences of the choices on the response menu.

When I was deep in the trenches of my political career, I laboured in a very divided society and emotionally charged atmosphere. I would visit districts where it would be probable I would be mingling with those who strenuously disagreed with my political policies and positions. From time to time, I would hear comments flung from the other side of the street or as I entered a building or facility. Ignoring this flack and chaff was, and is, the only sensible reaction to this shade of insult. At meetings and in the debating chamber, well, that was a different matter entirely, but scrapping in the street with the public wasn't my style, isn't a good look, and is seldom profitable. It should be avoided unless you are cornered with no way out. In some career choices, it comes with the job.

But occasionally, an especially tenacious critic would emerge from the shadows. In the face of their persistent barbs, I was afforded many opportunities to develop and test an effective counter-strategy. I think it is fair to explain that, from morning to evening, I was always accompanied by police protection, so I could be uncommonly brave while these trials were being conducted.

In my situation, which admittedly wasn't normal, my ground rules required me to keep moving, dodging potential opposition flash mobs like an agile gazelle. Nonetheless, when confronted, I found that a scathing reply did nothing to lessen the insulter's ire or of any audience to which the person might be playing. A witty response often served to keep a lid on the event and a sprinkling of self-deprecating humour helped me more and could even defuse the situation, akin to throwing cold water on a hot skillet.

Because of the security implications, it was unwise to dally in less welcoming territory, but smiling and making no response invariably left the detractor confused and frustrated. They would pause, wondering if I had heard their disparaging comment. They might, at this point, either disengage from further involvement (albeit using expletives as they parted), or try again, to make certain I didn't miss their invective. When met with more smiles and silence, the most intrepid of insulters might continue to harangue me with "You've no answer to that" or "Did you hear me?" This would be the point at which I would gently inform my antagonist: "I heard you the first time and I have already answered you." I would wait for the facial expression depicting puzzlement and incongruity to form, before adding, "I consider silence to be the best answer to your remark." However, as I took my "truth pill" this morning, I have to admit I had a range of extra lines, which were despatched depending on whether the person was particularly unpleasant or seriously obnoxious. (I concede that the rejoinder might, instead, have included a reference to a rat and the rear portion of its anatomy.)

As you can gather, I didn't go out of my way to avoid confrontation. It came to me; I didn't have to seek it.

Maybe it's just me, but I have always regarded the smart alec, who considered himself the sole authority on any topic, a tantalising fly, too good to resist swatting.

Over the years, I employed many attitude adjusters for this class of wise-guy. I discovered this species often dwell in colleges and universities. Here's one possible reply: "Really! That's what you think? Do you know that a snarky comment doesn't compensate for your intellectual shortcomings? Best to continue with your education and come back when you grow up. Just a friendly suggestion."

Enough of all that! Let's get back to the putdown response menu.

No First Strike

Amid the vast universe of social 'snubbery', our compass points towards an intriguing sector of this galaxy, spinning around the concept of the "No First Strike" policy in the world of putdowns.

The "No First Strike" policy could be typified as the gentleman's agreement of insult-trading. This means adopting the stance of the chuckle-making Chuck Norris, patiently waiting for an incoming kick before executing his countermove with aplomb and devastating timing. It neither means refusing to insult nor being meek. Instead, it embodies the proverb, "Everyone should be quick to listen, slow to speak," or in our context, "slow to roast". Our mission here isn't to plunge delicately balanced social situations into turbulence with unsolicited barbs; instead, we perfect our fortification until provoked, utilising putdowns and insults as counters and deterrents.

Exploring this policy exposes our shared humanity. We've all been present at an insufferable dinner party which, by its nature, involves a captive audience. Then some unfortunate soul becomes the prey of an uncle-in-law, emboldened after one too many sherries, who shoots off verbal volleys like a malfunctioning Roman candle. Dear Uncle's senses have been numbed by the sherry and the civility of the 'no first strike' rule has passed him by. But there's always that comedy hero who, waiting their turn patiently, lobs back a juicy retort, reducing the room to helpless laughter, granting sweet release from the tension. No harm, no foul; merely laughter echoing around, the memory of a wallop cushioned by timely humour (and the sherry).

There's a certain finesse, a dramatic artistry to delivering the perfect comeback. It's the joy of seeing someone adeptly filter raw rudeness, transforming it into a refined response, hilarious and intelligent. Akin to a skilled craftsman chiselling a snide comment into a sculpture of wit, a well-turned retort becomes a thing of beauty. The aim is to refine that raw artistry within us, always ready, never initiating.

Of course, a no-first-strike policy includes the essential element of timing, wrapped in a cloak of observation. It is a spectacle, requiring you to read your potential nemesis, listen to the rhythm of conversation, then fashion your strike with panache. When the insult comes, the response is not a vulgar counterpunch; it's a well-orchestrated jab, designed to disarm rather than harm. It subjects the initial offender to gentle public ridicule, a playful chastisement without serious rebuke, and provides the audience with a belly laugh and a story to retell.

Remember, this is where the frontier begins between defence and aggression: Let's not nuke them until nuked upon.

PLAY THE BALL, NOT THE MAN

The phrase "Play the ball, not the man" is fairly commonly used and originally comes from sport, specifically the game of soccer, where it advises participants to focus on the ball, rather than tackling the player. In broader usage, it is often employed metaphorically. In politics, business, and other situations, it means that one should focus on the problem at hand (the ball) rather than attacking the person involved (the man). So, if someone were to bring up another's past mistakes as a way of discrediting their argument, for example, they would be playing the man, not the ball. It advocates maintaining attention on the issue itself, and not indulging in mudslinging.

Of course, no such code applies in the territory of the 'exempt professions', which rely on verbal exchanges and duelling. Here, contestants know the rules (or know that there are none) and firing and dodging putdowns is just part of the contract. I say, do your worst and best. These discrete exceptions stray so far from socially acceptable rules that they can reach a crescendo, principally in politics where the name-calling often doesn't even come up to classroom levels. The use of a graphic appellation or a descriptive term attached to a person's authentic name is commonly used and typically draws attention to, and accentuates, an opponent's flaws. The best modern-day example is the "Sleepy Joe" reference used by President Donald Trump to frame a narrative around President Joe Biden. It gets repeated so frequently that the public then look for signs and confirmation of the failing when they watch President Biden.

Another example of playing the man rather than the ball is when someone's name is deliberately mispronounced. I had an opponent called Reg Empey, and in speeches and dialogue, my colleagues and I would refer to him as "Mr Empty". We would have claimed that this was a double whammy, in that it not only amusingly distorted his name, but also reflected how we evaluated his political calibre. The upside is that he could not complain without drawing more attention to the jibe.

Political activists in Scotland have used a similar tactic when referring to the Scottish National Party, First Minister, Humza Yousaf who they refer to as Humza Useless.

Outside the 'exempt professions', name-calling is predominately frowned upon and better avoided. Likewise, "playing the ball rather than the man" is regarded within the 'exempt professions' as both befitting and defendable.

JUST IGNORE IT

Many psychologists and philosophers will argue that silence is the best approach, and they will lecture all day and night about insult pacifism, quoting Stoic philosophers by the bucketful.

Stoic philosophers, such as Epictetus and Marcus Aurelius, believed in the importance of mastering one's emotions and maintaining inner peace. In the context of insults, Stoics advocated for a pacifist approach. Instead of reacting impulsively or seeking revenge, they encouraged individuals to respond with inner tranquillity and indifference towards insults. According to Stoic principles, insults held no power unless one allowed them to affect one's inner serenity. They emphasised the importance of virtue, self-control, and the understanding that insults are reflections of the insulter's character, rather than that of the one being insulted. Stoics believed that, by cultivating indifference towards insults, individuals could uphold their dignity and avoid unnecessary conflict.

Socrates, the renowned philosopher of ancient Greece, believed that responding to insults with reason and calmness was crucial. He taught that retribution for insults only perpetuates negativity, while responding with wisdom and understanding can lead to growth and resolution.

Confucius, the Chinese philosopher, emphasised the importance of restraint and dignity when facing insults. He taught that maintaining composure and treating others with respect, even when insulted, reflects one's inner strength and moral character.

Another prominent example is Aristotle, who discussed the nature of insults and their impact on human relationships. He believed that insults and abusive language could be damaging not only to individuals but also to the social fabric of a community. Aristotle emphasised the importance of using language wisely and advocated for respectful and civil discourse.

While it is difficult to make accurate computations about the views of modern-day philosophers, many contemporary philosophers draw upon these and other ancient philosophical traditions for inspiration.

Other modern-day philosophers argue that insult pacifism goes against our natural instincts to defend ourselves, both psychologically and socially. They believe it is important to engage in reasoned discourse and stand up against insults to protect our dignity and promote just treatment. Ultimately, philosophers hold diverse opinions on this topic, and their views can vary, based on their respective philosophical frameworks and perspectives.

While the perspectives from ancient philosophers offer insights into dealing with insults, focusing on self-control, rationality, and the cultivation of inner strength, their teachings are not always relevant and helpful in navigating such challenges today. Even more germane to this study is the reality that 99% of the population has never heard of their teachings.

Yet, there is sound common sense in much of what they say; if it is doable, why would you not rise above the insult and take the high ground? If there's no downside, other than not exacting your revenge, why not instead enjoy the power of silence?

I maintain that the crucial aspect is whether you have been, are being, or will be damaged by not responding. If it is only your pride that is the victim, and you can remain silent, the shame can only fall on the insulter, if you extract yourself with silence and grace.

WITTY SELF-DEPRECATING COMEBACKS

Wit has always been recognised as a powerful weapon, both in personal and professional interactions. The ability to use clever and amusing remarks to disarm opponents and influence outcomes can be a formidable skill. Lest it be considered that self-deprecation is a sign of weakness, it is important to understand that wit isn't about being mean-spirited or disrespectful. Instead, it is about leveraging one's intelligence and creativity to deliver sharp, incisive remarks that effectively challenge and expose others' flaws or assumptions. A skilled virtuoso knows how to strike the right balance between delivering a punch and maintaining a sense of humour.

When used effectively, it can serve as a defence mechanism, enabling individuals to navigate challenging situations with confidence. By poking fun at ourselves, we disarm our attackers and defuse the tension in the situation. It allows us to display poise, humility, and the ability to laugh at ourselves.

Firstly, self-deprecation implies that we don't take ourselves too seriously. By acknowledging our flaws and shortcomings with a touch of humour, we demonstrate that we're comfortable with who we are, and are not shaken by harsh words. This nonchalant attitude can throw our assailants off balance, making it harder for them to land a solid blow. It allows us to take control of the situation and takes away the power they might have had over us.

Besides disarming our opponents, self-deprecating humour also fosters a sense of connection with others. When we make light of our own imperfections, we create a relatable and approachable image. It shows that we aren't afraid to be vulnerable and that we understand what it feels like to struggle or make mistakes. This helps to build empathy and understanding between ourselves and those around us. When people see us respond to verbal attacks with grace and humour, they are more likely to view us in a positive light.

If someone who transparently opposes your views says:

 "You're off your rocker, everyone thinks you're mad."

Simply laugh and reply:

 "No, they don't! My invisible friend thinks I'm sane."

Abraham Lincoln, the great droll emancipator, was a master at using self-deprecating humour. On one occasion he disarmed an opponent who'd called him "two-faced", by replying:

 "If I had another face, do you think I'd be wearing this one?"

Self-deprecating humour can also act as a shield against criticism. By making fun of our personal perceived weaknesses or faults, we can take away the ammunition our attackers might use against us. For example, if someone were to criticise you for being clumsy, you could respond with a self-deprecating joke about your lack of coordination. By doing so, you redirect the focus away from the attack and put the spotlight back on yourself in a more light-hearted manner. This strategy can help to defuse the tension and make it difficult for attackers to persist in their verbal assault. When used effectively, self-deprecating humour can help us handle verbal attacks with confidence and grace.

 Ronald Reagan: *"I have left orders to be awakened at any time in case of a national emergency, even if I'm in a Cabinet meeting."*

However, remember that self-deprecating humour should be used judiciously and with care. While it can be an effective resource, it is essential to strike a balance between self-acceptance and self-mockery. If taken to extremes, it may undermine our self-confidence and confer the impression that we lack self-worth.

Not all situations can be navigated with self-deprecating humour, especially if the verbal attack is severe or deeply personal. In such cases, it may be appropriate to address the issue more directly.

If someone mocks your appearance:

 "You're absolutely right, I've put on so much weight. I hate it when I think I'm buying organic vegetables, but when I get home, I discover they're just regular doughnuts."

or,

 "I know, but I don't want to intimidate others with my good taste!"

or,

 "I don't care what people think of me. At least mosquitoes find me attractive."

If you are being teased because you're single:

 "Oh, I'm not single. I'm in a long-term relationship with fun and freedom."

or,

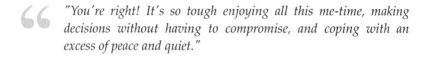 *"You're right! It's so tough enjoying all this me-time, making decisions without having to compromise, and coping with an excess of peace and quiet."*

or,

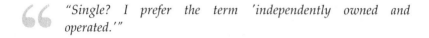 *"Single? I prefer the term 'independently owned and operated.'"*

or,

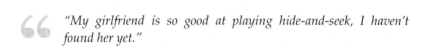 *"My girlfriend is so good at playing hide-and-seek, I haven't found her yet."*

DEFLECTION

Deflection can be an incredibly effective strategy when dealing with insults, serving as a form of emotional self-defence. It involves mentally sidestepping or changing the trajectory of an insult to avoid taking it personally or directly. This tactic could be used in various types of interpersonal interactions, including online communication, work relations, or personal relationships.

This tactic allows the recipient of an insult to maintain control, framing the interaction in a way that defuses conflict. Instead of triggering feelings of anger, frustration, or hurt, a deflection might respond with humour, change the topic, or address the insult indirectly. By shifting the narrative, deflection reframes the negative situation into something less confrontational.

However, it's important to note that deflection isn't about suppressing feelings. It is about not giving the intended negative impact of the insult any power over emotions or personal perceptions. This approach encourages resilience and emotional intelligence because it necessitates understanding one's emotions and managing them effectively.

Deflection doesn't mean avoiding conflict altogether. It often opens the possibility for an understanding or mature conversation with the offender. It bridges the gap, allowing dialogue to replace defensiveness. The key is knowing when and how to use this strategy appropriately, always considering the underlying motives of the person offering the insult and one's personal boundaries.

It is a delicate, non-aggressive reaction, which entails attempting to direct the insulter towards another subject or just acknowledging their position and asserting your own. Such responses regularly begin by following the flow of the putdown, but then move back to reaffirm the position previously taken. It is less combative and seeks to move the insulter's focus away from a hostile *modus operandi*. They don't need to contain humour and are absent of any crushing barbs. They do what it says on the tin – they deflect. Some examples:

> *"I appreciate your input, but I'll stick with my approach."*

> *"That's an interesting perspective, but I'm content with the path I've chosen."*

> *"I understand your point, but I find it more constructive to focus on solutions."*

> *"It seems like we have different ways of approaching things, and that's okay."*

> *"I'm always open to suggestions, but I ultimately trust my own judgement."*

> *"I appreciate your passion, but have you considered looking at it from another angle?"*

> *"I'm sorry if my calmness is confusing you, but I prefer to focus on productive conversations rather than arguments."*

> *"I admire your conviction, but I believe we can discuss this respectfully without resorting to personal attacks."*

Deflection techniques can also include the employment of diversion. This component of the art can be utilised to confound someone and leave them wondering what you meant by your response. One illustration if you are insulted is to smile while you are walking away and remark that:

> *"You need more prunes in your diet."*

" Comments that come out of left field and seem bizarre are reasonably sure to cause the aggressor to stop and try to decode your observation. Having received this advice, he may think that, as prunes are regarded as an effective laxative, you might be telling him he's full of... Alternatively, he might consider that, because the prune's properties play a role in lowering blood cholesterol by soaking up bile, you are suggesting his remarks had a bile-like quality. If he has any medical knowledge, he might be aware that a recent study has shown that prunes in a diet have excellent slimming benefits and you may be remarking on his girth. The advantage to you is that he will be spending his time wondering if he has been put down and in what way. Meanwhile, you will be sitting at home eating your dinner.

DEFUSE WITH HUMOUR AND CLEVER WORDPLAY

The use of humour and clever wordplay in defusing insults and putdowns is a tactic that lies at the heart of memorable and effective communication. Indeed, humour is more than just a vessel for jokes; it is a strategic tool, capable of transforming a tense or hostile situation into one that is considerably more light-hearted and manageable. Embracing the world of comedic retaliation can serve as a remarkable form of defence, and a testament to a person's mental agility and emotional intelligence.

Imagine finding yourself in a heated argument, where emotions are running high. Instead of resorting to aggressive or hurtful tactics, responding with well timed wit can defuse tension and steer the conversation towards a more constructive path. This witty repartee not only helps in resolving conflicts, but also ensures that relationships remain intact. In effect, wit becomes a cathartic release valve that transforms negative energy into something amusing and surprisingly insightful.

Besides providing a method that aids conflict resolution, satire can become a powerful device for persuasion. By presenting ideas or arguments in a clever and engaging manner, the person can capture attention and win over even the most sceptical of audiences. Wit allows individuals to put forth their stance with a charm and charisma that is as endearing as it is persuasive. It introduces an element of entertainment to conversations, making the message more memorable, appealing, and easier for others to connect with.

Creative insults and putdowns exemplify this approach. Composed of a delicate balance between language acuity and observational humour, they represent a linguistic art form, requiring a deep understanding of language, wordplay, and phrase-turning abilities. A creative insult isn't inherently hurtful or derogatory; rather, it's a humorous jab meant for mutual amusement more than anything. Phrases imbued with irony, embellishment or historic, cultural references make the exchange thought-provoking and engaging, converting what could be an exchange of hostility into playful banter.

Navigating between humour and offence is at the heart of a memorable putdown.

When used effectively, wit can serve as a defence mechanism, enabling individuals to navigate challenging situations with confidence.

By masterfully navigating between humour and offence, individuals can articulate their wisdom and emotional intelligence, fostering stronger connections through light-hearted and insightful communicative exchanges.

The world of politics is the classic model where wit can be put to use as a formidable weapon. Throughout history, politicians have used clever remarks and comebacks to assert their dominance, undermine opponents, and sway public opinion. The ability to turn a phrase or deliver a well timed punchline can generate a dramatic influence on the outcome of debates and even elections.

Playing with language, puns, and double entendres can turn a simple jab into a delightful linguistic movement. For example, instead of outright calling someone "stupid", you can reframe it with a creative twist, such as:

 "It's a good thing they invented Google for people like you!"

or,

 "I'm not saying you're stupid, but if brains were taxed, I'm sure you'd be eligible for a rebate."

Another aspect of creative insults is the ability to utilise irony and exaggeration. You can turn what could be an uncharitable insult into a hilarious observation. For instance, if someone calls you clumsy:

"Oh, you think I'm clumsy? Let's see you juggle life, charm, and wit as seamlessly as I do. Oh wait, I forgot, you'd need wit for that."

ENTER THE RING WITH A SHARPER RETORT

This takes us to a new level, where the atmosphere is different and the exchanges bear the unpleasant stench of disparaging remarks and gut-punching affronts. It's where verbal punches are exchanged, loaded with intent to provoke, ridicule, or hurt. There's no telling where it goes from this moment on. You might sense a distinct chill in the room. You haven't initiated the contest, but you are in intentional insult territory, where words serve as weapons, complete with bayonets of barbs.

Putdowns, when executed with finesse, can be a source of humour and playfulness in social interactions. But along comes the cheap-shot-slinger, intent on wounding dignity with insults purposefully loaded with venom.

The objective in your response should be to create laughter and foster a sense of camaraderie, but failing that, act like a heavyweight boxer, raining down punches left and right.

The best of insults has many fathers, so there's no certainty who first crafted this one. It is the story of a slightly intoxicated man approaching a seated gentleman and, while stroking his bald head, joking:

 "Your head feels just like my wife's bottom."

The quick-witted owner of the shiny dome stroked his head and mused,

 "Gosh, it does, doesn't it?"

Result – the insulter, insulted.

Timing is another crucial element. A well timed putdown can produce the desired comedic effect, while an ill-timed one might come across as mean-spirited or insensitive. Pay attention to the mood of the conversation and the dynamics within the group. If someone is already feeling down or vulnerable, it's best to refrain from using putdowns altogether.

Moreover, it's important to consider the nature and intensity of the putdown. Gentle teasing that highlights a harmless flaw or funny situation is more likely to be well received than a cutting remark aimed at someone's insecurities. Stick to benign topics that won't cause unnecessary discomfort or hurt feelings. Avoid personal attacks or anything that could touch on sensitive topics like appearance, intelligence, or private beliefs – unless you are counterpunching.

Another crucial aspect of putdown etiquette is to know your audience. Different people have different sensitivities and boundaries. While one person may enjoy a sharp-witted comeback, another may find it hurtful. Pay attention to how others respond to your putdowns and adjust your approach accordingly. If someone seems uncomfortable or becomes visibly upset, you need to recalibrate.

Be ready to apologise and make amends if the circumstances suggest it is necessary. Even the most well intentioned putdowns can sometimes miss the mark. If you unintentionally offend someone or realise that your putdown was inappropriate, an apology can go a long way in rectifying the situation. Taking responsibility for one's words demonstrates empathy and respect for others' feelings.

By considering the context, intention, timing, topic, and audience, we can engage in playful banter while still respecting the feelings of others. A well-executed putdown can be a source of laughter and bonding, but it requires tact and awareness to navigate the fine line between humour and offence.

SOME EXAMPLES OF CLEVER OR WITTY RESPONSES

"I see you're still committed to being the living proof that intelligence isn't hereditary."

"If I agreed with you, we'd both be wrong."

"You're like a broken compass – you have no direction and just keep going in circles."

"If they made a monument to ignorance, your face would be on it."

"I hope your failures give you the motivation to hit average someday."

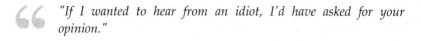

"If I wanted to hear from an idiot, I'd have asked for your opinion."

"I'm sorry for calling you 'stupid'. I thought you already knew."

"The trash gets picked up tomorrow. Be ready."

"Why not introduce your top lip to your bottom one?"

* * *

CYBER WARS – ONLINE PUTDOWNS

T he growth of the digital domain has only turned up the volume on this noise. Now, we have cyberbullies and trolls hosting packed concerts on social media platforms and in online forums, hurling insults like confetti, all hidden behind their handy invisibility cloaks.

The increase in digital traffic has amplified this exponentially. Cyberbullying and online trolling weaponise insults and offensive language to dominate discussions and debates. Shockingly, the vilest abuse is often directed at women in public life. The anonymity provided by the digital sphere emboldens users to tarnish and accost others, underlining a need to address this issue, particularly when it turns to abuse, threats and misogyny. It is a matter of dire concern as the internet becomes increasingly central to many aspects of our lives, such as communication, education, and entertainment.

Armed with anonymity, cyberbullying turns insults into virtual grenades, making the internet a battleground reminiscent of medieval jousting grounds – but with neither rules nor gallantry.

Here we discover two allotments that create fertile cultivating ground for insults to flourish like malicious weeds.

Social media putdowns are a prevalent form of interaction and expression on various online platforms. These quips are often used to criticise, insult, or belittle individuals or their ideas and beliefs. Let's explore this phenomenon further.

Social media putdowns can be categorised in many ways. There are *ad hominem* attacks, which involve attacking personal traits or someone's character, instead of addressing the argument or points directly. This behaviour should be scorned and regarded as a failure to counter the argument that has been advanced, because these personal attacks do not have a bearing on the validity of the opponent's argument. So, instead of arguing based on reason and evidence, the *ad hominem* approach uses personal criticism as an irrelevant distraction.

 "You're so stupid, I'm amazed you know how to use a keyboard."

This tweet is a personal insult and avoids engaging in a constructive conversation. It is at the softer end of the online barb spectrum, though it has the merit of including a mildly humorous element.

Another common approach is the sarcastic putdown. Sarcasm is often employed to mock or dismiss someone's viewpoint. An example could be:

 "Oh, congratulations! You've just shared the most unoriginal idea of the century."

The condescending tone and sarcastic remark are intended to undermine the person's input, making them feel invalidated.

Then we have the "keyboard warrior" putdowns. This occurs when individuals hide behind their computer screen and put others down. Dismissive comments such as–

 "You're just attention-seeking"

are common. Which is great coming from someone who wants to bring no attention to his or her anonymity. This type of response is designed to diminish others, while amplifying the aggressor's own sense of superiority.

Lastly, there are the backhanded compliments. On the surface, these putdowns carry an undertone of mockery or condescension. Examples include statements like–

"I admire your consistency, even though you're consistently wrong."

It starts with what appears to be a compliment but ends with a reverse sting.

Little is hurtful in the examples I have given – most fall within the "give and take" of social media exchanges; however, increasingly, the witty and clever insults are being smothered by their more offensive, vulgar, abusive, and threatening neighbours. As online discourse continues to evolve, if left unchecked, it will descend into a mire of such unpleasantness that no reputable human will want to visit.

Structurally, cyber insults can take several forms:

DIRECT ATTACKS

The person is overtly insulted or criticised, usually in a public setting or forum. This can be through derogatory comments, offensive memes, or targeted posts.

INDIRECT ATTACKS

This is subtler and can involve spreading rumours, passive aggressive comments, or veiled digs at the person in question. They may not appear offensive on the surface but imply negative connotations.

HARASSMENT OR STALKING

This includes persistent or orchestrated attacks against an individual over a period of time. Perpetrators may frequently post insulting content or make offensive remarks about the individual.

IMPERSONATION

The perpetrator may create false accounts and post offensive content while pretending to be the individual, damaging the person's reputation. Some fess up to being parody accounts, but others do not.

The nastiness of cyber insults continues its odious escalation as users — or perhaps more accurately, abusers — hide behind a veil of online anonymity, thus minimising accountability for their actions. This ominous echo chamber often spreads its message using very offensive, aggressive, or biased language, exuding forms of discrimination and imparting fake news.

In extreme cases, where the putdowns persist and escalate, it's essential to protect your mental well-being. Utilise platform features to report harassment or abusive behaviour, and when necessary, consider blocking the individual to maintain a healthy online space. No response is needed in this scenario; solely prioritise your own welfare.

In conclusion, understanding the structure, delivery, and evolution of cyber insults is the first step in devising effective countermeasures when confronted by over-the-top comments. It is helpful to remember you are participating in the "give and take" of – yes, "social" media.

SOCIAL MEDIA PUTDOWNS

"I'm jealous of people who haven't met you."

"I would roast you, but my mum said I'm not allowed to burn trash."

"Behind every great person, there's someone rolling their eyes."

"You're the reason they invented autocorrect."

"Do yourself a favour and delete your account. It's for the best, trust me."

"I'm sorry, I didn't mean to hurt your feelings. I meant to hurt your entire existence."

"You're like a chemical reaction – two parts dumb and one part delusional."

"Do you ever wonder what life would be like if you'd gotten enough oxygen at birth?"

"I'm sorry, did my eye-roll interrupt your irrelevant opinion?"

"*They say honesty is the best policy, so I'll be honest. You're annoying.*"

"*Sarcasm is just one more service I offer.*"

"*Do you ever wonder if your parents liked you, or do they just pretend for your birthday?*"

"*You're not a complete idiot – some parts are missing.*"

"*I'll never forget the first time we met – but I'll keep trying.*"

* * *

WITTY TECHNIQUES FOR HUMOROUS INSULTS

I n much of life, comebacks and insults are without humour, though, in my view, the best ones will pay homage to the custom. Wordplay's linguistic wizardry can be practised to entertain, engage, and even insult – if dispensed with a dose of humour, it has added value. It gains an entertainment bonus and can give a measure of protection to the user from the downside blowback of being insensitive or nasty.

In the realm of clever wordplay, putdowns become not so much hurtful jabs, they transform into witty repartee, leaving both speaker and recipient mildly amused – unless, of course, the recipient's pride is more fragile than a porcelain teacup. If you aspire to master the art of humorous insults, read on, and discover some witty techniques for clever wordplay.

One technique that stands out in the world of humorous insults is the use of irony laced with a sprinkle of sarcasm. What an adrenaline-charged concoction – the bittersweet yin and yang of the insult world. These elements bring a sense of absurdity to an insult, making it both amusing and thought-provoking. For instance, declaring:

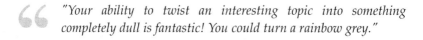 *"Your ability to twist an interesting topic into something completely dull is fantastic! You could turn a rainbow grey."*

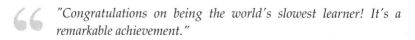 *"Congratulations on being the world's slowest learner! It's a remarkable achievement."*

Such sarcasm-laden compliments showcase the absurdity of insulting someone by applauding their less-than-stellar qualities. But why stop there? Ponder upon these –

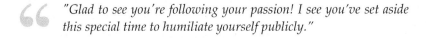 *"Glad to see you're following your passion! I see you've set aside this special time to humiliate yourself publicly."*

"Oh, I see you've mastered the art of wearing mismatched socks. You're a fashion trendsetter!"

Here, the insulter's pinnacle of achievement is unexpectedly acclaimed, but only for its unintentional or undesired failing.

Yet beware! Even the finest gladiator in the Colosseum of wit is likely to have the gauntlet thrown down by an adversary whose ambition is to enthral the spectators with the brilliance of their oratorical wit and thereby raise their sword triumphantly over your limp cadaver. If you are the victim of someone else's humorous putdown, and you're up for it, the imperative involves a quick, seamless-as-silk, retort. If you take a "hit", silence will give your foe a shiny victory, so fire back with whatever you have. Always be armed with a comeback locked and loaded in your reprisal revolver – you never know when you might need it.

The best seemingly unscripted, spontaneous, impromptu, and extemporaneous ripostes can be carefully planned, polished, and practised well in advance. However, as you can never predict what the features of an attack may be, you can only prepare a generic response (or a holding response while you put your brains into gear). You might say:

"Wow, well done, your sense of humour is truly out of this world. It's like you're from a planet where jokes go to die."

Here, the comeback uses irony and sarcasm. It is couched in irony by praising someone for their peculiar sense of humour, and adding a touch of sarcasm by implying that it is unfunny and unrelatable. Most important, it gives you thinking time to recover. So, prepare, but never over-prepare. Let your wit flow like a river, carrying you to the shores of victory.

Additionally, exaggeration can be a powerful tool in crafting humorous insults. By amplifying a person's flaws or quirks to astronomical proportions, you create playful hyperbole that evokes laughter instead of offence:

"You're so slow, your shadow leaves you behind!"

or,

"Your ego is so big; it needs its own postal (zip) code!".

Journalist Paul Taylor stretched the limits of this category when referring to Peter O'Toole's appearance:

"Peter O'Toole had a face not so much lived in, as infested."

These over-the-top statements capture the essence of their shortcomings while maintaining a jovial tone.

Or why not try the reversal technique? Flipping meanings and associations like a pancake brings forth a fresh viewpoint to insult delivery. Picture these:

"He's so dull, he could put Ovaltine to sleep,"

or,

"You're so reliable when it comes to getting directions. When you ask your satnav to take you home, you end up at the lost and found."

or,

"Congratulations, you've managed to reach impressive levels of mediocrity!"

Lastly, why not pour some rhymes and alliteration into the cauldron of wordplay? Crafting insults with a musical quality creates a symphony of memorable and engaging repartee. For example:

"Where's the fire, where's the zest? Your pitiful prose puts minds to rest."

"Your attire screams fashion disaster from a mile away; it's like a catwalk catastrophe,"

which showcase either a rhyming effect or an alliteration, making the insult not only clever but also catchy.

While these techniques can make your insults more amusing, it's crucial to remember that they often work best when conveyed with a wicked smile and delivered with a sense of impishness. Gauge the recipient's reaction and ensure your words are taken in the spirit you intended – whether that's one notch below a gentle jibe or one above the robust level.

Whatever path you chose, clever wordplay offers a doorway to inject humour into insults, sprinkling them with wit and charm. Puns, irony, sarcasm, exaggeration, reversal, alliteration, and rhyming hold the keys to transforming a simple insult into a remarkable, mirthful exchange. Practise these techniques with a light touch, and you'll master the art of delivering humorous insults with the least downside blowback after the laughter fades.

* * *

Putdowns From the World of Books

I nsults in literature are not limited to reality, but also include fantasy, dystopia, and other genres.

Memorable Classic Literature Putdowns

Classic literature is filled with memorable characters, each with their unique voice and opinions. Within the pages of these cherished books, readers have come across some of the most scathing and unforgettable putdowns ever penned. From biting comebacks to cutting remarks, these literary gems have left an indelible mark on readers for generations.

One iconic example can be found in Jane Austen's beloved novel, 'Pride and Prejudice'. This literary masterpiece gives us a famous putdown, delivered by the sharp-tongued Elizabeth Bennet to the snobbish Mr Darcy.

Darcy: *"She is tolerable; but not handsome enough to tempt me,"*

Elizabeth: *"I could easily forgive his pride if he had not mortified mine."*

This exchange perfectly captures the wit and intelligence for which Austen's characters are known.

Moving on to Charles Dickens's 'A Tale of Two Cities', we encounter the enigmatic Sydney Carton. In an emotional scene, Carton delivers one of literature's most heart-wrenching self-putdowns. When he confesses his unrequited love for Lucie Manette, he reveals his own despair and self-deprecation:

 "I am a disappointed drudge, Sir. I care for no man on earth, and no man on earth cares for me."

This cadence and poignancy of this self-deprecation makes for a powerful moment that leaves a lasting impact on the reader's heart.

In the realm of tragedy, William Shakespeare is both bard and master of the barb. His works present a treasure trove of memorable putdowns, with perhaps the most famous one found in 'Romeo and Juliet'. Mercutio, the quick-witted friend of Romeo, unleashes a scathing tirade, where he mercilessly mocks Romeo's romantic notions:

 "Romeo, the love I bear thee can afford no better term than this: thou art a villain."

This biting insult reminds us that best friends can deliver the harshest blows when love and passion are at stake.

Taking a detour to the world of fantasy, Tolkien's 'The Lord of the Rings' provides us with another impressive putdown. In a moment of bravery and defiance, Eowyn, the shield-maiden of Rohan, confronts the witch king of Angmar. When he arrogantly states,

 "No man can kill me,"

Eowyn unveils her true identity and delivers a memorable retort:

 "I am no man."

This simple yet powerful line showcases Eowyn's strength and challenges the gender norms of her time.

Lastly, we must not forget the wit and wisdom of Oscar Wilde. His plays and novels are stuffed with countless spectacular putdowns, but none are as sharp as Lady Bracknell's words in 'The Importance of Being Earnest'.

When Jack Worthing tries to propose to Gwendolen, Lady Bracknell responds with icy precision:

"To speak frankly, I am not in favour of long engagements. They give people the opportunity of finding out each other's character before marriage."

This cutting remark captures the satirical nature of Wilde's work and leaves readers chuckling at the audacity of the characters. He was not alone in perfecting that art.

"None has ever wished it longer."

— SAMUEL JOHNSON ON JOHN MILTON'S PARADISE LOST.

"He would make a lovely corpse."

— CHARLES DICKENS

The world of books holds a treasure trove of memorable putdowns that continue to captivate readers. From Austen to Wilde, the wit and insight of these literary giants have immortalised some of the most biting and clever retorts ever conceived. These putdowns not only entertain but also offer a unique glimpse into the human condition and the power of words. So, next time you delve into the world of classic literature, keep an eye open for those unforgettable moments, testifying to the enduring nature of literary genius.

Modern-day authors have also developed a unique knack for integrating putdowns and barbs into their character interactions, painstakingly weaving them into narratives. This creative strategy serves to add depth and realism to the characters, thereby enhancing the reader's experience. These elements find their roots in the authors' ability to understand human nature, dynamics, drama, and humour and use it as a tool to engage readers.

The use of putdowns and insults in contemporary literature can serve a variety of purposes. Sometimes, it's a means to develop a character's personality or to emphasise a specific trait. These traits often mirror everyday social interactions, thus making the characters more relatable and human. For example, an author may employ a witty taunt to portray a character's intelligence, sharp tongue, or high social status. On the other hand, the target of the insult could be depicted as submissive, weak, or discomforted, thereby creating a certain power dynamic.

Authors like J. K. Rowling, George R. R. Martin, and Gillian Flynn have mastered the art of crafting memorable insults and comebacks. For instance, Rowling's character Draco Malfoy in the 'Harry Potter' series often uses putdowns to emphasise his perceived superior status. Meanwhile, Martin's key figures in 'Game of Thrones' use insults to assert dominance, display cunning, and manipulate others. Flynn's characters in 'Gone Girl' etch out their dark and complex personalities, using sharp, biting words as their weapons.

Moreover, the skilful employment of putdowns and insults often adds to the inherent humour, sarcasm, or satire of a piece, making it more appealing to the reader. They become pivotal not only in driving the plot forward, but also in detailing the complexities of inter-character relations. In some narratives, these elements can even serve to comment on or mirror broader societal hierarchies and prejudices.

Creating effective putdowns and insults that don't come off as forced or overdone requires a good understanding of language, timing, and character development. The best modern-day authors are those who deftly weave these elements into their stories to create compelling narratives that resonate with readers.

The vilest of insults from the pen of authors seem to be reserved for "their own kind".

 "The affair between Margot Asquith and Margot Asquith will live as one of the prettiest love stories in all literature."

— DOROTHY PARKER

 "I loathe you. You revolt me, festering in your consumption. You are a loathsome reptile – I hope you die."

— D. H. LAWRENCE TO ONE-TIME FRIEND AND WRITER KATHERINE MANSFIELD

> *"Nature, not content with denying him the ability to think, has endowed him with the ability to write."*

— A. E. Houseman, Poet

> *"His imagination resembles the wings of an ostrich. It enabled him to run, though not to soar."*

— Thomas Babington Macaulay, Historian on John Dryden, Poet

> *"I never converse with a man who has written more than he has read."*

— Attributed to several 18-century writers

> *"Your manuscript is both good and original; but the part that is good is not original, and the part that is original is not good."*

— Samuel Johnston is credited as saying this but it is questionable if he was the originator

Putdowns in Literature and From Writers

> *"It was very good of God to let Thomas Carlyle and Mrs Carlyle marry one another and so make only two people miserable instead of four."*

— Samuel Butler, Novelist

> *"Oh, really! What exactly is she reading?"*

— Dame Edith Evans on hearing that novelist Nancy Mitford was overseas finishing her book

> *"If it were thought that anything I wrote was influenced by Robert Frost, I would shred it and flush it down the toilet, hoping not to clog the pipes."*

— James Dickey

"The stupid person's idea of a clever person."

— ELIZABETH BOWEN ABOUT ALDOUS HUXLEY

"She's the sort of woman who lives for others; you can tell the others by their hunted expression."

— C. S. LEWIS, THE SCREWTAPE LETTERS

"He has no enemies, but is intensely disliked by his friends."

— OSCAR WILDE, ON BERNARD SHAW

"He has a face like a constipated bulldog, and he combs his hair with a live squirrel."

— P. G. WODEHOUSE

"He's a man of great common sense and good taste, meaning thereby a man without originality or moral courage."

— GEORGE BERNARD SHAW, ABOUT CAESAR

"He has the attention span of asparagus."

— TERRY PRATCHETT

"He's as smart as bait."

— DOROTHY PARKER

"He's never in a hurry except when he's going nowhere."

— TRUMAN CAPOTE

"Gibbon's style is detestable; but it is not the worst thing about him."

— SAMUEL COLERIDGE, POET, ON HISTORIAN EDWARD GIBBON

"*He reached rock bottom and started to dig.*"

— Douglas Adams

"*If you had another brain, it would be lonely.*"

— Dorothy Parker

"*He is simply a hole in the air.*"

"*He's the reason they invented the phrase 'intellectually challenged'.*"

"*He's like a blind man in a dark room looking for a black cat that isn't there.*"

"*He's the kind of person who can sit on a fence and yet manage to fall off on both sides.*"

"*He has the brain of a gnat and the attention span of a goldfish.*"

"*His mouth moved faster than an auctioneer on caffeine.*"

"*His wit is so subtle; it could sneak past an army of pun detectors.*"

"*He almost danced to the fridge, found the three least hairy things in it, put them on a plate and watched them intently for two minutes. Since they made no attempt to move within that time, he called them breakfast and ate them.*"

Putdowns in Comic Books

"*You're like a broken pencil – pointless and constantly needing sharpener.*"

"*Did it hurt when you fell from mediocrity?*"

"*You have the charm of a landfill on a hot summer day.*"

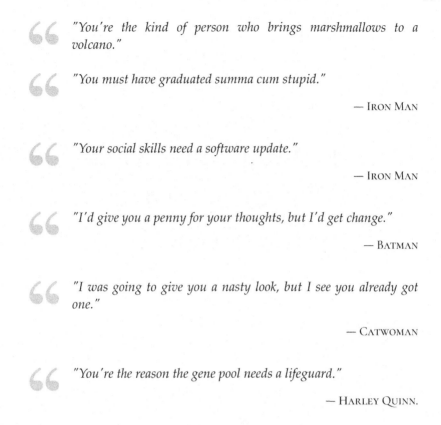

"You're the kind of person who brings marshmallows to a volcano."

"You must have graduated summa cum stupid."

— IRON MAN

"Your social skills need a software update."

— IRON MAN

"I'd give you a penny for your thoughts, but I'd get change."

— BATMAN

"I was going to give you a nasty look, but I see you already got one."

— CATWOMAN

"You're the reason the gene pool needs a lifeguard."

— HARLEY QUINN.

* * *

THE CULTURAL
CONTEXT OF
PUTDOWNS

Our journey now brings us to the social narratives that define insults and putdowns. Cultural conventions categorically influence what one perceives as an insult and the level of acceptance towards demeaning language. Some traditions readily employ what may be perceived as "an abhorrent affront" in others, as spirited banter, while some observe strict codes of respect and formality.

In the captivating realm of national idiosyncrasies, the spectrum of putdowns and their level of acceptance is broader than the hues of a sprawling rainforest. Certain cultures generously sprinkle what others might perceive as insults, within their witty exchanges, akin to a grandmother sweetening her home-baked cookies with sugar. Conversely, there are those who adhere to a strict Victorian standard of etiquette, reminiscent of Emily Post, where not even the slightest hint of an insult is allowed to escape.

Cultural variations can be a complex labyrinth to navigate. The explorer must recognise the importance of following a route that avoids the IEDs of diversity in style, level of directness, and potential societal implications.

As tour guide, I can alert those who interact with people from different backgrounds to the fact that there are instances when and where "you're silly" is friendly joshing and times when it is an existential wound. These perspectives reconfigure like a buffet, some going gung-ho on banter and oxymorons, while others consider respect as sacred as grandma's secret recipe.

The canned laughter we hear on screens when quick-witted, insulting characters trade verbal blows have perhaps muddled our actual admin panel settings. We may need a reboot before those staged shenanigans become indistinguishable from real-life consequences.

We know that putdowns, or insults, are a universal aspect of human communication. They serve to assert dominance, establish social hierarchies, and express dissatisfaction. However, the form and cultural context in which a putdown is used can vary significantly across different regions and backgrounds.

In Western cultures, particularly in English-speaking countries, putdowns frequently employ sarcasm, irony, and clever wordplay. They value wit and linguistic dexterity, aiming to ridicule cleverly or provoke a laugh. For example, one might hear phrases like,

   "You're as useful as a screen door on a submarine"

or

   "He's about as sharp as a bowling ball."

These remarks focus on humour, effectively pointing out the perceived incompetence or foolishness of the person being insulted.

In contrast, East Asian cultures, such as Japan and China, tend to prioritise indirectness and subtlety in their putdowns. Face-saving and preserving harmony within the community are important values. Therefore, insults are conveyed more implicitly, often through euphemisms or metaphors. For instance, a Japanese insult might involve calling somebody "paper-thin", implying that they lack depth or substance.

Regional and ethnic backgrounds within Western cultures can also shape the style of putdowns. In the United States, for example, humour is frequently employed, and putdowns may be more direct and confrontational. They can playfully mock someone's intelligence, appearance, or behaviour.

However, it is essential to be mindful to avoid sensitive topics or transgressing acceptable boundaries, especially if you are a visitor in foreign territory or the guest in the domain of a different cultural group. In the United Kingdom, putdowns typically rely on sarcasm, irony, and self-deprecation to critique others subtly.

Moving beyond Western and East Asian contexts, different cultures have unique ways of expressing putdowns. In Middle Eastern and African cultures, for instance, it is common to employ metaphors and analogies to criticise or mock someone indirectly.

Middle Eastern Cultures:

Arabic – "You're like a mirror." This saying indicates that a person changes and adapts too much, depending on the situation or the people around them, losing their originality.

Turkish – "An empty word does not sail a cheese ship." I am uncertain of the origin of this quote, but it is used to emphasise that talk alone doesn't get any work done; indicative of someone being all talk and no action.

African Cultures:

Swahili – "Giving birth to a child is not a task, the task is raising them." Often used to criticise someone who has initiated a project but failed in their responsibility to see it through properly.

Amharic (Ethiopia) – "In the house of a thief, when you judge, you rule the kingdom." This is used to suggest that someone is making a big deal out of a small or petty issue.

Yoruba (Nigeria) – "If you are not financially prepared by the time trouble arrives, you're bound to eat porridge." This is a criticism of someone for being unprepared for a foreseeable issue.

It is always important to remember that context is key, and direct translation might not carry the full depth or intention of the cultural meaning behind such sayings. They can also depend on the region, dialect, and many nuanced factors for true understanding.

This approach allows for the delivery of sharp and critical remarks, while still maintaining politeness and avoiding open conflict. The underlying cultural emphasis on hospitality and respect often shapes the way putdowns are delivered in these contexts.

It is worth mentioning that the cultural context of putdowns isn't static. Since Biblical times, insults have been part of a human's repertoire. But they have evolved over time, influenced by globalisation and the increasing interconnectedness of societies. As people from diverse backgrounds interact and share cultural knowledge, the lines between regions and backgrounds have begun to blur. Additionally, the rise of social media and the internet, along with the vast distribution of movies and television programmes, is leading towards a greater harmonisation. This has given rise to a new form of putdown culture, where memes, trolling, and snarky comments thrive.

Until cultures merge, care will still be required, lest we fall into inadvertently offending the cultural values others hold. Being respectful and aware of cultural nuances is essential in avoiding misunderstandings and building cross-cultural relationships.

Falling into the pit of unintended consequences can result from cultural differences. Listeners may become bemused or offended and the speaker confused as to the cause of the stir he has provoked. Words employed routinely and in normal speech in one tradition may translate into a derogatory term when heard in another culture.

In Western cultures, asking someone's age, especially a woman's, can be considered disrespectful, due to societal stigma around age. However, in many Asian cultures like Korea and China, asking someone's age is not only acceptable, but often necessary early in the conversation, to be able to use the correct form of address, accommodating their hierarchical language structures, based on age and status.

In America, accepting a compliment with a thankful acknowledgement is the norm. Whereas in East Asian cultures, including Japan and China, it's customary to self-deprecate or refuse a compliment to demonstrate humility.

"Pardon my French" is an American English phrase, used to excuse the speaker's use of swear words or, more broadly, when a speaker has said something crass. However, in French-speaking countries, this might be perceived as rude or offensive, because it implies that the French language or culture is associated with vulgarity.

In the United States, the term "fanny" is often used to denote the backside or buttocks and is considered a very casual term. It is used regularly when referring to a fanny pack, which is a small fabric pouch secured with a zipper and worn with a strap around the hips or waist. However, in the UK, Australia, and New Zealand, "fanny" is a vulgar slang term for female genitalia. Using it jovially or casually in these regions, as one might in the US, may cause discomfort or offence.

Cultural context can be critical. It emphasises the importance of cultural sensitivity, especially for public figures, politicians, and diplomats. Taking the time to understand and respect the cultural nuances and sensitivities of various communities isn't wasted time. You would avoid using the phrase "killing two birds with one stone" if you were addressing the Royal Society for the Protection of Birds. Wouldn't you?

In conclusion, putdowns across different regions and backgrounds vary significantly in terms of style, directness, and standards. Whether it's the witty banter of the West, the subtlety of East Asia, or the indirectness of the Middle East, insults reflect the social dynamics and ethics of the communities where they originate. Appreciating and understanding the underlying cultural values and social dynamics is crucial in interpreting and using putdowns appropriately. This acknowledgment should help readers navigate the potential pitfalls of cultural misunderstandings or unintentionally causing offence.

* * *

PUTDOWNS IN EVERYDAY LIFE

Dealing with challenging interactions in everyday life can often be difficult, especially when confronted with insulters. Their remarks or actions are intended to belittle, criticise, or undermine others. Whether they occur in the workplace, social settings, or even within personal relationships, manoeuvring in these situations requires tact and resilience.

These trysts can cause emotional distress, damage relationships, and undermine our self-esteem, thus making it worthwhile to explore the concept and provide strategies for coping with such encounters.

It's crucial to remain calm and composed when faced with a jibe. Reacting impulsively or aggressively might escalate the situation further. Take a deep breath and remind yourself not to take the remark personally.

Remember, putdowns often reflect the insecurities or frustrations of the person delivering them.

You will recall that the most effective strategy in dealing with putdowns is to use humour. A well-placed joke or light-hearted response can defuse tension and disarm the person delivering the putdown. For example, if someone mocks your appearance, you can cleverly respond with something like:

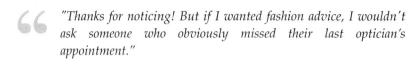

"Thanks for noticing! But if I wanted fashion advice, I wouldn't ask someone who obviously missed their last optician's appointment."

If someone who lives for themselves were to disrespect your dog:

Narcissist: *"I don't like dogs; I have no time for them."*

Response: *"You should buy one, since they're the only creatures who will love you more than you love yourself."*

Then there is the quick return used by Pierre Trudeau when responding to an insult:

"I've been called worse things by better people."

Using humour demonstrates your ability to maintain confidence and not let the remark impact your self-esteem. There are occasions when a personal tease can be spoken, and no offence is taken.

I am sure this would be the case at a wedding, when everyone (except the father of the bride who has watched everyone dining on his dime) is in fine form and having a great time. You are posing for a group photo. The gregarious photographer jestingly berates the bride's father:

"George, you're making my job more difficult. The sun is reflecting off your head."

Unless he is ultra-sensitive, everyone will laugh, and the victim might respond:

"I'm paying for a photographer, not a second-rate comedian"

or

"I hope you're a better photographer than you are a comedian."

Playful banter is part of social interaction, and we have all — except for the dullest and most po-faced — participated in it.

Another approach, if the words are more cutting, is to privately confront the putdown directly but assertively. Calmly explain how the comment made you feel and why it was inappropriate. Expressing yourself in a non-confrontational manner can help create open dialogue and potentially lead to a resolution or even remorse. By addressing the issue head-on, you assert your boundaries and let the other person know their behaviour is unacceptable.

In some situations, ignoring the putdown may be the best approach. Some people deploy putdowns to seek attention or provoke a reaction. By refusing to engage and choosing not to give their comments any credence, you take away their power. Maintain your composure, carry on with your activities, and let their words roll off your back.

Building self-confidence and cultivating a strong sense of self-worth are crucial in handling putdowns. People who are secure in their abilities and value themselves are less likely to be affected by negative comments. Focus on your strengths, achievements, and the positive aspects of your life.

Remember that your worth is not determined by the opinions of others.

In challenging situations, it's important to surround yourself with a supportive network of family, friends, or colleagues who uplift and encourage you. Share your experiences with trusted individuals who can provide guidance or lend a listening ear. Having a strong support system can help bolster your resilience and provide perspective.

I once heard about a lesson employed frequently by a life coach. Standing before his pupils, he takes a five-dollar bill from his pocket, and asks the class, "Who wants this?" The class response is immediate – all the hands go up. He crumples it up, crushes it between his hands and asks, "Who wants it now?" The hands all go up again. Then he tosses it violently to the floor, stands on it repeatedly and asks once more, "Who wants it now?" Again, he is faced with a sea of enthusiastic students, with hands raised. "Why?" he asks a young girl at the front of the class. "Because it's worth five dollars," she replies. "Exactly," he says. "No matter how you are crushed and stood upon in life, you don't lose your value."

Your worth is not determined by the unkind words of others, and you have the power to rise above negativity and cultivate healthier, more positive relationships. It's essential to recognise when a putdown becomes a pattern of abuse or bullying. If someone consistently puts you down, undermines your abilities, or engages in manipulative behaviour, it may be necessary to reassess the relationship. Establish clear boundaries, and if the behaviour persists, consider distancing yourself or seeking professional help to navigate the situation.

In conclusion, dealing with putdowns in everyday life can be perplexing, but it is possible to respond in a constructive and empowering manner. Remember to remain calm, consider using humour, and confront the dig assertively when necessary. Focus on building self-confidence, seek support from loved ones, and recognise when a putdown crosses the line into abuse. By employing these strategies, you can handle challenging interactions with grace and maintain your emotional well-being.

INSULTS ON T-SHIRTS

It is safe to assume that someone who ventures into the public space with a messaged t-shirt wants it read by friends and passers-by. They clearly are intent on communicating something about themselves or their opinions to those they meet or whose path they cross. The message may be projected towards others, but often it is about their personality, views, desires, or physical features. The message's purpose will be to make people smile, think, or even to shock them. Most will be light-hearted and intended to raise amusement:

 "I'M NOT FAT, I'M JUST EASY TO SEE."

Some provoke thought, but the message may be too complex for someone to grasp in five seconds, while walking past in the street:

 "FI UOY NAC DAER SIHT RUOY TNEGILLETNI EKIL EM!!"

Others are just rude and offensive and may even be used to clear the pavement, as decent people will cross the street. I will resist giving an example – just take a walk downtown.

A word of caution to the fairer sex; be aware that, if you wear messaged t-shirts, you will draw glances or gazes from a lot of guys at a part of your anatomy which differs from theirs. So, if you are sensitive, keep your message short.

THE IRRITATING WORKPLACE SMART ALEC

This can be a challenging task. However, once again, a witty response can help you effectively handle such situations, while maintaining a sense of professionalism. These clever comebacks can not only disarm the loudmouth, but also bring a smile to the faces of others present. Let's delve into some witty putdowns that can come in handy when dealing with such individuals.

> "I'm impressed with your ability to talk so much without saying anything of substance. It's a true talent!"

> "Your one-liners are legendary. It's just a shame the rest of your work doesn't live up to the same standard."

> "Well, at least your jokes provide some comic relief. It's the only thing you seem to excel at!"

> "I must admit, your sharp tongue is quite impressive. It's a shame it's not accompanied by a sharp mind."

> "Your ability to find humour in everything is truly commendable. It's a shame it doesn't translate into problem-solving skills."

Do use these putdowns sparingly and with caution. While they can be effective in maintaining your dignity and dealing with a workplace gasbag, it's essential to strike the right balance between humour and professionalism. Ultimately, the goal is to defuse tense situations, while promoting a positive and respectful work environment.

Always keep in mind that perspective is everything. Context and tone are crucial when using witty rejoinders. It's important to maintain a balance between defusing the matter with humour and avoiding sarcasm or mockery, which may further escalate tensions. Adapt a variation of these examples to suit your situation and ensure they align with maintaining a constructive and respectful conversation. Maintain your composure and avoid responding with aggression. Reacting in kind could escalate the situation further. Take a moment to reflect, remain calm, and remember that you have control over your own emotions and behaviour.

Active listening is a valuable skill when dealing with a babbler. Give them your undivided attention and listen to what they have to say, even if their tone is hostile. This demonstrates respect and can help defuse the tension. Acknowledge their perspective and show that you are genuinely interested in understanding their concerns.

Empathy can also play a crucial role in defusing a situation. Try to put yourself in their shoes and understand the underlying emotions driving their behaviour. This doesn't mean condoning their aggressive actions, but showing empathy may help you find common ground or identify potential triggers you can address calmly.

When responding to a confrontational loudmouth, assertiveness is key. Stand your ground and communicate your thoughts and boundaries clearly and confidently. Use "I" statements to express your feelings without coming across as confrontational. For example, instead of saying, *"You're wrong,"* try saying, *"I see things differently."* This approach fosters open dialogue and encourages respect.

Distancing yourself from the situation is sometimes necessary. If the display of agitation becomes overwhelming, it's okay to take a step back and create some physical or emotional space. This can provide an opportunity for both parties to cool down and reflect on the situation. It may also allow you to approach the issue with a fresh perspective later.

Another technique is to redirect the conversation towards more positive or productive topics. If the windbag is fixated on a negative subject, try shifting the focus to a shared interest or a more constructive aspect of the discussion. By doing so, you can steer the conversation away from potential conflict and create a more amicable atmosphere.

Additionally, choosing your battles wisely is important. Not every disagreement is worthy of engagement. Sometimes, it's best to let a comment slide if it's not directly affecting you or the people around you. By picking your battles carefully, you can conserve your energy for situations that truly warrant your attention and response.

Lastly, it might be beneficial to seek support from others who may have experience dealing with similar individuals. Discussing strategies, venting, or seeking guidance can provide you with valuable insights and coping mechanisms.

Remember, dealing with such situations requires patience, empathy, and assertiveness. By maintaining your composure, actively listening, and responding with clarity and respect, you can navigate these conditions more effectively.

However, if the braggart is incorrigible, perhaps they need a lesson to take them down a notch.

PUTDOWNS FOR EVERYWHERE AND EVERY DAY

"If only he washed his neck, I'd wring it."

— JOHN SPARROW.

"If looks could kill, you'd be a weapon of mass destruction."

"Of course, I'll help you out. The same way you came in."

"I may look calm, but in my mind, I've killed you 20 times, in the last five minutes, in 20 different ways."

"I'm trying to imagine you with a personality."

"It's amazing how you can constantly hit new levels of mediocrity."

"They say he is his own worst enemy. Not while I'm alive!"

"Selfish? He would unplug your life support machine to charge his phone."

Nosy neighbour: *"Hey, what's up? Washing your car?"*

Reply: *"No, I'm watering it to see if it'll grow into a bus."*

"When I'm feeling down and someone says, "suck it up", I get the urge to break their legs and say, "walk it off".

"If your phone doesn't ring, it's me."

"Sorry. Did the middle of my sentence interrupt the beginning of yours?"

INSULTING A PERSON'S APPEARANCE OR INTELLIGENCE

> *"That's the kind of face you hang on your door in Africa."*
>
> — JOAN RIVERS ON DONATELLA VERSACE

> *"You look good when your eyes are closed, but you look even better when mine are closed."*

> *"Mirrors can't talk; lucky for you, they can't laugh either."*

> *"I would explain it to you, but I have neither the time nor the crayons."*

> *"I'm not saying you're dumb; you just have bad luck when thinking."*

> *"Light travels faster than sound. This is why you seem to be bright until you speak."*

> *"I'd challenge you to a battle of wits, but I see you came unarmed."*

> *"Zombies eat brains. Don't worry, you'll be safe."*

> *"If I wanted to hear from an idiot, I'd have asked for your opinion."*

> *"I see you're still committed to being the living proof that intelligence isn't hereditary."*

> *"If I agreed with you, we'd both be wrong."*

> *"In his defence, he was left unsupervised."*

QUEUE-JUMPER PUTDOWNS

> *"Excuse me, I didn't realise we were playing musical chairs. The line starts over there."*

"I think your GPS must be broken. The back of the line is that way!"

"Guess you didn't get the memo; we're pretending to be civilised here."

"The line-skipping championships is next week."

"Didn't realise we were playing leapfrog. Still, your turn's back there."

"Your ticket to the express line seems to have been misplaced. Please join the line like the rest of us."

"Pardon me, were you looking for the line or the limelight?"

PUTDOWNS IN THE WORKPLACE

"They say laughter is the best medicine, which makes you the workplace's unofficial pharmacist."

"I'm amazed by your ability to turn any team meeting into a personal monologue."

"Your ability to make simple instructions seem like ancient hieroglyphics is truly remarkable."

"I'm sorry, I didn't realise the company hired a professional comedian."

"I'm busy right now, can I ignore you some other time?"

"Is there a support group for people who have to work with you?"

"You're the reason they invented the phrase 'lost cause.'"

"If there were an award for doing the bare minimum, you'd still manage to come in second."

Putdowns Used in Sport

John Motson was my favourite sports commentator. He demonstrated a keen intellect:

> *"The World Cup is a truly international event."*

He had an ability to evaluate and share valuable information to the viewer:

> *"It's Arsenal 0 – Everton 1, and the longer it stays like, that the more you've got to fancy Everton."*

But above all, he was a man who was sensitive and avoided courting controversy:

> *"I think this could be our best victory over Germany since the war."*

Managers, sportsmen and sportswomen, but particularly referees, become the target of many *sporting putdowns*:

> *"Ally McLeod thinks tactics are a new kind of mint."*
>
> — Billy Connolly on the Scotland manager

> *"The only time Nick Faldo opens his mouth is to change his feet."*
>
> — David Feherty, golfer and golf commentator

> *"I know why Boycott's bought a house by the sea – so he'll be able to go for a walk on the water."*
>
> — Fred Trueman, Cricketer

> *"Howard Cosell was gonna be a boxer when he was a kid, only they couldn't find a mouthpiece big enough."*
>
> — Muhammad Ali

"*I've seen George Foreman shadow-boxing, and the shadow won.*"

— Muhammad Ali

"*We must have had 99 percent of the game. It was the other three percent that cost us the match.*"

— Chelsea manager Ruud Gullit after a defeat.

Let the Terraces Speak

"*Do you need a GPS to find the goal?*"

"*If tripping over yourself were a crime, you'd be serving a life sentence.*"

"*If mistakes were points, you'd be the reigning champion.*"

"*Hey, ref, if you had one more eye, you'd be a cyclops!*"

"*You run like you're trying not to spill your tea!*"

"*I've two goldfish that swim faster than you!*"

"*Hey! The ball called; it's feeling lonely!*"

"*Ref! Did you leave your guide dog at home?*"

"*Hey, ref, did you not read the manual that came with your whistle?*"

"*With all those missed calls, you should be working for a voicemail service!*"

Conflict-Avoiding Responses to Putdowns

Putdown: "*You're such a failure.*"

Response: "*I appreciate your concern, but I'm confident in my abilities and I'm focused on improvement.*"

Putdown: *"You'll never amount to anything."*

Response: *"We all have different paths, and I'm excited to explore mine. Thanks for your input."*

Putdown: *"You're way too sensitive."*

Response: *"I believe having empathy and being in tune with my emotions is a strength. It allows me to connect with others on a deeper level."*

Putdown: *"You're always so indecisive."*

Response: *"I take my time to carefully consider my options. It helps me make better decisions in the long run."*

Putdown: *"You're so naive."*

Response: *"I prefer to see the good in people and situations. It keeps me optimistic and open-minded."*

Putdown: *"You're just lucky; it's not a skill."*

Response: *"Yes, the more skilled I get, the luckier I am. I've worked hard to achieve my goals and develop my abilities."*

Putdown: *"You're always taking the easy way out."*

Response: *"I strive to find efficient and effective solutions. It's about working with people, not putting them down."*

RESPONSES TO VERBAL ATTACKS

"Is that the best insult you could come up with? Bless your heart."

"Well, aren't you a little ray of sarcasm?"

"I see your IQ test came back negative."

"You're lacking in originality just as much as you're lacking in basic manners."

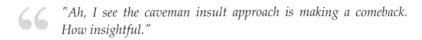

"Ah, I see the caveman insult approach is making a comeback. How insightful."

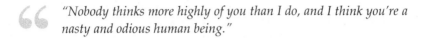

"Nobody thinks more highly of you than I do, and I think you're a nasty and odious human being."

MEDICAL PUTDOWNS

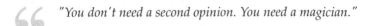

"You don't need a second opinion. You need a magician."

"I'd guess your speciality isn't bedside manners."

"No, I don't snore. I dream I'm a chainsaw to scare away boring doctors."

"Do you charge per pill or per mistake?"

SCHOLARLY WIT

"The highlight of your essay was your name."

"You're the 'Ctrl-Z' of our workgroup, undoing every bit of progress."

"I'm not sure what you're studying, but it certainly doesn't seem like our subject."

"If distractions were a metric, you'd be the class topper."

"Your eagerness to answer the question is inversely proportional to your accuracy."

"Seems your schedule planner came without the 'study' option."

"If only you attacked your homework like you do your lunch."

THE CHURCH

" *"It's no accident that the symbol of a bishop is a crook, and the sign of an archbishop is a double-cross."*

— GREGORY DIX, ANGLICAN MONK

" *"Confession on Saturday. Absolution on Sunday. At it again on Monday."*

— H. G. WELLS, WRITER, ON CATHOLICS

" *"I feel like a lion in a den of Daniels."*

— ORIGINALLY ATTRIBUTED TO OSCAR WILDE, WHO AT TIMES FACED CLERICAL CENSURE FOR HIS LIFESTYLE. OTHERS INSIST THE COMMENT WAS MADE BY WILLIAM S. GILBERT.

* * *

CONCLUSION

Y ou will have gleaned that I am not a putdown pacifist. But I do recommend adhering to a code.

We have talked about how some vocations use linguistic combat as part of everyday functioning. In these distinctive and specialised careers, the rules of etiquette and civility often take second place to delivering a message that will be retained in the audience's memory or to the key objective of winning and succeeding. These I have called the 'exempt professions'. Yet even in these cage-fight environments, wit and humour trump venom and abuse. In the heat of battle, when the blood is bubbling, it is easy to exceed the limits of what is appropriate – now, looking back, I'm sure I overindulged on occasion. A psychological analysis might insinuate that, in part, writing this book is self-flagellating penance for those times. In case any of my former victims take solace from this suggestion, I say, "Not a bit of it. I am unrepentant. You all deserved what you got, except perhaps. . ."

In the non-exempt realm, decent people will, for the most part, follow a code that adopts a "No first strike" policy. They will refrain from biting back at inadvertent offenders and avoid attacking the defenceless. Equally important, they will choose putdown responses commensurate with the attack suffered and use wit or clever wordplay when possible. Unless it is unavoidable, they will "play the ball and not the man" and if all else fails, then they'll remove the gloves.

To keep my lawyers happy (if such were ever possible) I should give you a warning. If the person you are hoping to "get one over on" weighs 280 pounds, is six feet eight inches tall, sports evil-looking tats, a scowl, and a square jaw, then you need a back-up plan – or three. I suggest you don't deploy an insult unless someone is around to transport you to the hospital. Smile profusely, in the hope that he is either appeased or as dumb as he is broad and might interpret your putdown as a compliment. Of course, go right ahead if you're an accomplished sprinter.

 I don't reimburse medical bills, so use your new skill wisely.

— THE AUTHOR

* * *

Book Review
Witty Putdowns and Clever Insults
You can make a difference!

Hey there, your help is needed for a truly noble cause. I'm not asking for your lunch money, but requesting something even more valuable: your honest review!

You may be wondering, what's the big deal about leaving a review? Well, let me share a secret with you. Most people judge a book by its cover (and its reviews). A cleverly crafted review, like a well-executed jab, can make all the difference. Your words have the power to help someone discover the book's hidden gems.

But let me tell you something even more extraordinary. Your gift costs no money and takes less than 60 seconds to make a real impact. Yet, it can help someone in ways we cannot even begin to imagine.

So, let's join forces, dust off your keyboard. Your review is the gift that keeps on giving, and with it, you'll be spreading joy and unlocking the power of wit and wisdom. Thank you in advance for your generous act of reviewing. Remember, even the smallest words can make a big impact!

CREATE A REVIEW
eBook Readers - Click the link below to leave your review on Amazon.
https://www.amazon.com/review/review-your-purchases/?asin=
B0CN55QQP2

Paperback and Hardcover Readers can scan the QR Code.

Printed by Amazon Italia Logistica S.r.l.
Torrazza Piemonte (TO), Italy

53554882R00077